Ethnic Options

Choosing Identities
in America

Mary C. Waters

UNIVERSITY OF CALIFORNIA PRESS
Berkeley · Los Angeles · Oxford

University of California Press
Berkeley and Los Angeles, California

University of California Press, Ltd.
Oxford, England

© 1990 by
The Regents of the University of California

Library of Congress Cataloging-in-Publication Data

Waters, Mary C.
    Ethnic options: choosing identities in America / Mary C. Waters.
      p. cm.
    Includes bibliographical references.
    ISBN 0-520-06856-4 (alk. paper).—ISBN 0-520-07083-6 (pbk.
alk. paper)
    1. Ethnicity—United States. 2. United States—Population.
I. Title.
E184.A1W29 1990
305.8′00973—dc20
                                       89-49150
                                         CIP

Printed in the United States of America
     4   5 6   7   8 9

The paper used in this publication meets the minimum requirements
of American National Standard for Information Sciences—Permanence
of Paper for Printed Library Materials, ANSI Z39.48-1984 ⊚™

077431

Ethnic Options

For my mother and father

Contents

Tables

Preface

This book, like many before it, is the result of a puzzle that surfaced when its author was working on an earlier project. One day in 1984 Stanley Lieberson and I were conducting a detailed review of tables of numbers the computer had spewed forth after going through five magnetic tapes containing a sample of the 1980 census. The figures we were looking at contained data from the ancestry question on the 1980 census form and compared people who had reported various ancestries and combinations of ancestries in terms of a variety of socioeconomic indicators. Thus, for example, we were comparing the incomes of people who said they were of Italian descent with those who said they were of Polish descent, or with those who said they were Italian-Polish or German-Irish-English. In interpreting the data and comparing the numbers, Stan and I kept getting involved in questions the numbers could not answer to our satisfaction. Questions like, what does it mean to be both Italian and Polish? If you have both of those ancestries, do you feel closer to one or the other? Did the people who said simply that they were of German descent really have no other ancestries in their backgrounds? What about people who said they were American? Did they know where their ancestors were from and just not want to say? How would families with varied ethnic backgrounds and lots of ancestries choose among them to answer the question? What did a question about ancestry mean to people? If people did identify a specific ancestry, did it make any difference in their lives? Did the aggregate numbers we were comparing describe groups, statistical categories, or merely individual whims?

One thing that became clear from the data was that there was an awful lot of flux going on among these later-generation Americans—intermarriage was high, parents were not giving the same ancestry for their children as for themselves, and reinterview studies indicated that some people were changing their minds about their ancestry from survey to survey. I believe that most things sociologists ask about in censuses and surveys are complicated, and that good survey researchers should think about what is going on behind the scenes, but this issue seemed to me to be even more complex and interesting than most. How did people come up with an answer to a question on ethnicity, and did their answers have much meaning at all?

Discussing these issues, Stan and I ended up in effect interviewing each other about what we would say to the census. Stan is Jewish, which presents problems right away, because the census does not accept religion as an answer to the ancestry question. His wife is part English and Scottish. Stan began telling me what he knew about where his parents were from and began wondering what he would answer for his children, since they had a mix of ancestries; what they would answer if they were to fill out the form; and what his wife would answer if she were asked. I, too, began to talk about how I would answer the question—my four grandparents were all immigrants from Ireland, and the census question accepted Irish as a response, so in a way I didn't appear to have many choices. But as Stan and I talked, it became clear that even my apparently straightforward Irish ethnic identity had some twists to it. First of all, I had always been annoyed at people who made a big deal about being Irish—especially on Saint Patrick's Day and I began to wonder whether filling out the form on a census day just a few weeks after Saint Patrick's Day might have made me think of just saying American. Sometimes I am tempted to just say American when people ask, especially when I think I might be lumped together with people I don't necessarily consider to be authentically Irish. When Stan pointed out to me that Irish on the census form would include both Irish Catholics and a good proportion of Irish Protestants, I really began to wonder what I would have said, since I had always considered these to be very separate groups.

The more Stan and I worked with the data and analyses, which would become our monograph *From Many Strands: Ethnic and Racial*

Groups in Contemporary America, the more we wondered about the process that went on before the question on ancestry was answered, and in general about the role of ethnicity among later-generation whites in America. We reached the conclusion that someone ought to talk to some "regular people" in depth about this. So, with Stan's encouragement, I abandoned my previous dissertation topic, bought a tape recorder, learned about interviewing, and set out in search of some regular people.

This is the story of what I learned about the process of answering the census question on ancestry, about ethnicity in general, and ultimately about American culture and ideology, from talking to some very nice regular people in suburbs of San Jose and Philadelphia. I learned that Stan and I were not alone in having long and sometimes surprising stories behind our answers to questions about our ethnic backgrounds—stories that reveal the fascinating history of American immigration and ethnic assimilation, but that also reveal aspects of our own shared American culture and ideology—our shared values of individualism and community and the unique ways in which ethnic identities fulfill very American needs. I also learned that ethnicity is still a complex and changing subject, which still has real political and social consequences in shaping American thinking about race relations. Finally, I learned that combining quantitative and qualitative research techniques is an endeavor that, while difficult and time-consuming, is rewarding and productive. The interviews allowed me to pursue some interesting questions generated by looking at aggregate census data, and the patterns available in census and survey data suggested questions and areas to ask people about in the the interviews. Some sociologists have described quantitative and qualitative approaches as being somehow inherently antagonistic, but I have found them to be very complementary. The census gives us a picture of the relative size and characteristics of ethnic ancestries in the country as a whole, and the interviews give us some suggestions about the processes behind the identities and about the meanings people attach to them. Together these investigations suggest that ethnicity in America is an endlessly fascinating and constantly changing phenomenon.

Acknowledgments

There are people who love to spend their days by themselves writing books, but I am not one of them. I find that it is a lonely and sometimes frightening thing to do. As a result I never would have been able to do it without the emotional and intellectual support of family, friends, teachers, and students. This book exists because I have been blessed with a large and wonderful supply of all of them.

Stanley Lieberson encouraged and guided this project from its very beginning. It was in conversation with him that the idea was born, and from that moment on he provided wise counsel, cheerful encouragement, useful and supportive criticism, and unfailing humor and accessibility. Christine Williams read every word of every draft of this book with interest, enthusiasm, and keen sociological insight. She had just the right blend of discouragement for my long and wordy digressions, and encouragement for my often hidden ideas. Her red pen was a terrific help throughout the process, but especially with the final manuscript. Since these acknowledgments are the only part of the book that escaped her watchful and ruthless eye, the reader can judge from their length how unwieldy the book would have been without her. Judy Auerbach also endured countless early drafts and provided much advice, criticism, and enthusiasm and good spirits along the way.

I am very grateful to the many others who also took the time to read or comment on all or part of the manuscript, including Avi Chomsky, Steve Cornell, Joan Fujimura, Andrew Greeley, Gene Hammel, Brian Powers, David Riesman, Theda Skocpol, Neil Smelser, Terry Strathman, and Laurie Wermuth. The late Carol Hatch spent hours discussing this project with me; her enthusiasm for it periodically re-energized mine, and her acute questions and observations strengthened the argument. I have also benefited from discussions with Michael Meranze, Dan Greenberg, Dana Takagi, and Kwok Kian Woon.

This work was supported at the University of California, Berkeley, by a grant from the Chancellor's Patent Fund, the Survey Research Center, and through a NICHD Trainee Grant through the graduate Group in Demography. In addition to financial support, the Graduate Group in Demography also provided a community of researchers and an intellectually stimulating environment. I am grateful to Ron Lee, Ken Wachter, and Gene Hammel for the center they have created. While he was not directly involved with this project, I would like to acknowledge the important influence of Kenneth Bock on my development as a sociologist and a teacher. I have looked to him as an example of a committed, principled, and moral teacher and scholar.

At Harvard I received financial support from the Clark Fund for Faculty Research, and the Faculty Aid Program. Jennifer Hall and Kim McClain, and Maggi Apollon provided wonderful research assistance. The students in my courses on ethnicity gave me fresh perspectives and lots of new knowledge and energy.

Many others provided support in the countless details that go into a project of this kind. Ward Bell provided computer programming help when I desperately needed it. Chris Lorenz provided a much-needed transcribing machine. Borgna Bruner did a superb editing job. Priscilla Preston transcribed some interviews, and Suzanne Washington helped in the preparation of the final manuscript. Michelle Barbour helped me very much in the initial stages of this project. I very much appreciate her kindness and enthusiasm, as well as that of her whole family, especially Jackie Barbour. Naomi Schneider of the University of California Press was encouraging from the beginning, patient in the middle years, and very helpful in the final stages.

My friends literally and figuratively sustained me throughout this project with love, humor, dinners, home-brew, and most of all, the telephone. Thanks especially to Helen Schwartz, Bahaa Fam, Carol Nowacki, Sanday Waxman, François Ramarason, Julie Liss, Matt

Dennis, Terry Strathman, Kwok Kian Woon, Ang Ying-Hung, Martin Button, Steve Cornell, Lucia Benaquisto, Steve Rytina, Ellen Wojahn, Rita Chang, Laurie Wermuth, and Rachel Fershko.

I am very grateful to the people I interviewed. They gave freely of their time, their memories, and a small portion of their lives.

My family has been a terrific source of emotional support as well as cheap labor. My mother read the entire manuscript twice with editorial advice, helpful suggestions, and her characteristic love and unlimited time for her children. My father's keen observations on ethnicity in Brooklyn, especially as applied to distinctive driving techniques, most surely sparked my interest in this subject at an early age. Both of my parents' love of learning and storytelling prepared me well for this project. My sister Margaret read the manuscript and edited it thoroughly. She made my work breaks both fun and nourishing by bringing many cups of coffee and soup to my office and by providing amusing non-academic entertainment as I consumed them. My brother John and my sister Joan traded time on the transcribing machines for California vacations. My brother Tommy explained an important and highly technical aspect of car maintenance to me, without which I would not have been able to get to my interviews. My other brothers and sisters, Mike, Anne, and Liz, as well as my sisters-in-law Sheila and Mary Kay and my brother-in-law Joel provided emotional support and encouragement in countless other ways.

Finally, and in a category all his own, Nicholas R. Nova deserves a lot of praise. He stuck with me throughout this project. He never had a breakdown, nervous or the other kind, and except for a few minor occasions when it was snowing, always went where I told him to go.

CHAPTER 1

Introduction

In the first decades of the twentieth century the United States experienced massive immigration from Europe—especially southern and eastern Europe. The sheer numbers of these immigrants and the fact that many of them came from illiterate peasant backgrounds made the task of assimilating them into American life seem overwhelming. The degree of discrimination against them and their children and the amount of isolation they experienced in urban ethnic ghettos threatened to keep them forever separate from the "core American culture."

Immigrants and their absorption were thus an important political and social issue, and in the young and developing academic field of sociology, they became a focus of scholarly interest. Sociologists conducted valuable field studies of the ethnic ghettos in major American cities and theorized about the process of adaptation and assimilation in American life. The idea behind these theories was that with more time in America—more generations in the United States—the groups would become more assimilated—more Americanized.

The very success of the assimilation process these sociologists described makes it difficult for us to imagine the degree to which the question of the immigrant's eventual assimilation was indeed an open one. While the United States had absorbed immigrants from northern and western Europe through the eighteenth and nineteenth centuries, the immigrants from southern and central Europe, who started arriving in great numbers around 1870, faced harsh conditions and a great deal of prejudice and discrimination. Leonard Dinnerstein and David M. Reimers describe the degree to which these immigrants and their children were despised and excluded:

> Italians...were one of the most despised groups. Old-stock Americans called them wops, dagos, and guineas and referred to them as the "Chinese of Europe" and "just as bad as the Negroes." In the South some Italians were forced to attend all-black schools, and in both the North and the South they were victimized by brutality. In 1875 the *New York Times* thought it "perhaps hopeless to think of civilizing them, or keeping them in order, except by the arm of the law."

Greeks and Poles were also not given a warm welcome:

> The new immigrants were stereotyped as representatives of some kind of lower species...Greeks were physically attacked in Omaha,' Nebraska, and they were forced out of Mountain View, Idaho. A New Englander, observing some Poles weeding rows of onions, commented: "Animals, they work under the sun and in the dirt; with stolid, stupid faces." (Dinnerstein and Reimers 1982, 36)

These new European immigrants were seen by many as a "race" apart and were certainly described in racial terms:

> It is fair to say that the blood now being injected into the veins of our people is "sub-common."...You are struck by the fact that from ten to twenty percent are hirsute, low-browed, big-faced persons of obviously low mentality. Not that they suggest evil. They simply look out of place in black clothes and stiff collar, since clearly they belong in skins, in wattled huts at the close of the Great Ice Age. (Ross 1914; 285–86)

> "The Slavs," remarks a physician, "are immune to certain kinds of dirt. They can stand what would kill a white man." (ibid., 291)

We all know that the situation has changed for these immigrants and their descendants. The historical process of those changes—the adaptation and assimilation of these immigrants and their gradual full acceptance into American society—was a subject of study by generations of American sociologists. Through ethnographic studies in ethnic ghettos, as well as social surveys and analyses of American attitudes, sociologists have chronicled the assimilation process for these vast waves of European immigrants and their children and grandchildren. As a result of these studies we have learned a great deal about ethnicity, ethnic groups, and ethnic identity. We know how immigrants who came to the United States gathered in ethnic neighborhoods, created ethnic voluntary organizations, and imparted to their sons and daughters the old traditions and identifications of their past lives. We also know that ethnic identity and the vitality of the ethnic group decline in importance when the structural reasons for the maintenance of ethnic identity—such as discrimination, residential segregation, and strong religious identification—decline.

However, since the time of the original interest and theorizing done by sociologists about American ethnic groups, the number of immigrants from Europe has dwindled and the nature of American white ethnic groups has changed. In the 1920s restrictive immigration laws drastically cut immigration from all sources—especially southern and eastern Europe. As a result the groups that were so troubling and challenging to some Americans—Catholics and Jews from southern and central Europe—reduced their new members to just a trickle. This has affected the generational distribution of people of European origin in the United States. In each decade since the cutoff in European immigration in the 1920s, the population of European origin has aged generationally. Today the overwhelming majority of white ethnics of European extraction are third-, fourth-, and later-generation Americans.

The success and social mobility of the grandchildren and great-grandchildren of that massive wave of immigrants from Europe has been called "The Ethnic Miracle" (Greeley 1976). They are doctors, lawyers, entertainers, academics, governors, presidential and vice presidential candidates, and Supreme Court justices. But contrary to what some of the theorists and politicians predicted or hoped for, these successful and mobile 1980s Americans have not completely given up ethnic identity. Instead, they have maintained some connection with their immigrant ancestor's identities—becoming Irish-American doctors, Italian-American Supreme Court justices, and Greek-American presidential candidates. In the tradition of our cultural pluralism, successful middle-class Americans in the late twentieth century maintain some degree of identity with their ethnic backgrounds.

In fact, precisely when the descendants of the turn-of-the-century immigrants were moving into the third and later generations and experiencing more social mobility than ever before—in the 1960s and 1970s—there were many academics and popular writers challenging the predictions made earlier that ethnicity would decline in importance. The publication of Nathan Glazer and Daniel Patrick Moynihan's *Beyond the Melting Pot* in 1963 was a watershed event, opening a debate that raged for the next few decades over whether ethnicity would ever disappear as a powerful political and social force in American life.

The academic debate over whether Americans would ever lose their ethnic identities in the melting pot was characterized as one between the "assimilationist" and "pluralist" perspectives on ethnicity (Yancey et al. 1976). The assimilationist school argued that for later generations of Americans, further removed in time from the original immigrants, ties to the ethnic group are increasingly less important.[1] They point out that the structural forces that maintain ethnic group solidarity and cohesiveness have been waning. The declining residential segregation of white ethnic groups, declining occupational specialization, increasing intermarriage, social mobility, and distance in time and generations from the original immigrants all decrease the isolation of the ethnic group that has maintained its cohesiveness. As the descendants of the original immigrants leave the ethnically homogeneous ghettos of urban areas, it is argued, their social world is increasingly ethnically mixed and their ties to the original ethnic culture are reduced. Without political or economic reasons for maintaining ethnic solidarity, the importance of ethnic identification and allegiance for the individual *declines* and other means of identification and political and economic organization *develop* (Hechter 1978). For instance, if occupations are increasingly assigned in the society based on more universalistic criteria, such as ability and education, instead of the ascriptive criterion of ethnic origin, individuals will identify increasingly with class or status characteristics rather than ethnic ones.

The crucial factor for writers in the assimilationist perspective is the degree of structural assimilation of members of the ethnic group. Milton Gordon argues that acculturation can take place as immigrants and their children adopt the culture of America, but that ethnic groups cannot survive structural assimilation. As long as the world of primary relationships—neighborhood, friendships, and marriage— remains ethnically homogeneous, the salience of ethnicity remains strong. Once the world of primary groups becomes ethnically heterogeneous, however, assimilation proceeds and the ethnic groups begin

1. This expectation was the product of the influential work done by sociologists in the Chicago School (Park and Burgess 1925; Wirth 1928). Thus, for example, Park's diffusion theory suggests that assimilation should occur as a function of length of residence in the United States (Park 1950).

to disappear (Gordon 1964). Following this logic, the suburbs were predicted to be the great mixer of immigrants and their children because the move away from the ethnic neighborhood increases the chances that friendships and other close associations will occur with people from outside the ethnic group.

The pluralist perspective, on the other hand, argues that ethnic assimilation is *not* inevitable. Andrew Greeley (1971, 1974) and Michael Novak (1973), for example, challenge the concept that the importance of ethnicity necessarily rests on continued ethnic segregation within the broader society. Greeley argues that even when such primary relationships as ethnic intermarriage occur, there is still evidence that ethnic identity is maintained. He points to continued high endogamy rates, continued socioeconomic and attitudinal differences among ethnic groups even into the third and fourth generations, and continued self-identification of individuals as ethnics on sample surveys as evidence that assimilation is not imminent. The continued ethnic identification of suburbanites is also cited as evidence that ethnic cultures do not automatically disappear with the move away from traditional urban neighborhoods (Cohen 1977, 998; Agocs 1981). For instance, Winnetka, Illinois, attracts Chicago's upwardly mobile Irish-Americans, while other suburbs such as Oak Park attract newly rich Poles.

This debate between proponents of the melting pot and those of cultural pluralism in the 1960s and 1970s was fueled in part by developments among white ethnics of European origin, but was also very much a result of the new wave of largely non-European immigrants ushered in by changes in the immigration law in 1965—as well as by the experience of the civil rights movement and the general political mobilization of America's racial minorities.

The question of whether ethnicity would cease to matter for the later generation was assumed to provide an answer to what would eventually happen to the new wave of non-white immigrants and what could happen to the newly empowered—but long-time American—blacks, Indians, and Chicanos.

Some analysts argued that the success of these earlier immigrants was a reason to welcome diversity in our immigrant streams—pointing out that the xenophobic fears of the 1920s were unfounded, and in fact seem ridiculous from the vantage point of today. Other writers used the success of the descendants of European immigrants to oppose programs such as affirmative action and the Voting Rights Act, arguing that if the European ethnics could achieve social mobility with no government help, none was needed for America's racial minorities.

These debates were all based on an assumption—only sometimes made explicit—that what happened to white immigrants from Europe would provide a model or a comparison point for the experience of other ethnic and racial groups. In fact, the models of assimilation and cultural pluralism used by American sociologists were developed based on the experiences of these European groups—and especially important in these models is the concept of movement through generations. The further removed in generations from the earlier immigrants, the more assimilated the descendants would be.

Thus the debate that began in the 1960s and 1970s about the relative importance of ethnicity for groups of European origin had a great deal of significance. Theoretically it was important because it extended our knowledge of the processes of ethnic assimilation. The general models of assimilation based on these white ethnic groups made definite predictions about the later generations. If these predictions were not coming true, some argued, we needed to reexamine our general theories about ethnicity in America. Politically and socially it was also a crucial question. Since the generational distribution of Italians, Irish, Poles, and others in the United States was increasingly concentrated in later generations, the issue was one of real survival for these groups, and there was much emotion on all sides of the debate. If fourth-generation Italian-Americans ceased being "Italian" in any meaningful sense, and ceased identifying as Italian, then white European ethnicity was reaching the end of the road in the United States.

THE NEW ETHNICITY

Several theories emerged in the 1970s as it became clear to both assimilationists and pluralists that some type of ethnicity was persisting in suburban areas and among the middle class. Some analysts trivialized the importance of this "new ethnicity." At one extreme, Howard Stein and Robert Hill (1977) argued that Americans of later generations and of mixed ancestry had what they call "dime store ethnicity." That is, they can choose a grandparent to identify with and thus become symbolically a descendant of that group, much as one might shop for a product in a dime store. Stein and Hill distinguish that sort of "unreal" ethnicity from what they character-ize as "real" ethnics among this same population. The "dime store ethnics" are fake because they consciously choose an ethnicity and parade it in public. The "real ethnics" are real precisely because they are not conscious of the subtle influence their ethnic heritage con-tinues to assert in their daily lives.

Other writers recognize that while ethnicity has not been so im-portant in people's lives as it once was, it is not a trivial or unreal phenomenon. Morton Weinfeld (1981, 79) points out that even with-out group political or social activity, individuals can have a very real and meaningful attachment to an ethnic collectivity, which may manifest itself as a symbolic attachment to a remembered phrase, a favorite song, or some other small symbol of a remembered past. Richard Coleman and Lee Rainwater (1978, 111) argue that ethnicity adds spice to an otherwise bland postindustrial existence, and that ethnic identity is important to people because "it gives a sense of heritage and roots to a highly mobile population." If people no longer perceive a threat to their individual life chances from ethnic discrimi-nation, their ethnic identity can be used at will and discarded when its psychological or social purpose is fulfilled.

In an influential article on this subject, Herbert Gans (1979) addresses this central issue of what the continued identification of whites with an ethnicity, seemingly in isolation from a wider ethnic group, can mean. He suggests that later-generation white ethnics may have merely a "symbolic identification" with their ancestry. He views this symbolic identification as more or less a leisure-time activity. Individuals identify as Irish, for example, on occasions such as Saint Patrick's Day, on family holidays, or for vacations. In other words, for later-generation white ethnics, ethnicity is not something that influ-ences their lives unless they *want* it to. In the world of work and school and neighborhood, individuals do not have to admit to being ethnic unless they choose to. Ethnicity has become a subjective identity, invoked at will by the individual. Yet its very subjectivity and voluntary character lead to fundamental questions about its future viability, given increasing intermarriage and the resulting mixed an-cestries in people's backgrounds. Gans also wonders how such sym-bolic ethnicity can continue when the actual ethnic collectivity that the individual claims to belong to continues to recede. When a fourth-generation individual of Italian heritage tries to "be Italian," where does his or her notion of what being Italian means come from?

Are media images of Italians providing the only role models or "collectivities" with which to identify?

These writers made some interesting suggestions about the nature of ethnicity among later-generation individuals that bridge the gap between the assimilationist and pluralist perspectives. Theorists of a "new" or "situational" ethnicity try to explain the existence of middle-class, suburban later-generation ethnic identity: the ethnicity that the assimilationists predicted should not exist anymore in any meaningful sense, and that the pluralists argued meant quite a lot in ways that might be hard to measure or document. But these theories contain more conjecture and theorizing than hard evidence, in part because the population at the heart of the debate—suburban, middle-class later-generation descendants of European immigrants—is difficult to reach. The very suburbanization and social mobility that assimilation theorists predicted would undermine ethnic identity also make it much more difficult for researchers to study this population.

The rich texture of life in ethnic ghettos has been chronicled through participant-observation studies seeking to explain and explore the life of the ethnic group. Studies such as Gans's *The Urban Villagers* (1962), a portrait of Boston's Italian West End, describe situations in which the ethnic group and ties of ethnicity were still quite salient for individuals. But the suburbanization of white ethnics in the 1980s makes it difficult, if not impossible, to assess their ethnic identities through the types of field studies done in Little Italy or Polish urban neighborhoods in the 1920s to the 1960s. Scattered in suburbs and working in jobs that are not assigned on the basis of ethnicity, the majority of the descendants of the European immigrants cannot easily be studied through a study of neighborhood groups. Sociologists interested in white ethnics of European extraction have had to change both their methods and their focus of study. Instead of their studying the "ethnic group" as a collectivity, attention has shifted to the "ethnic identity" of the individual, and instead of participant observation and field methods, the sample survey has become the preferred research tool.

MEASURING ETHNIC IDENTITY

The information we have about later-generation ethnicity in the 1980s comes from studies that rely on "ethnic identification" of individuals of later generations in national sample surveys such as the

General Social Survey (GSS) of the National Opinion Research Center (NORC); the National Survey of American Catholics in 1963; and political and voting studies that ask for ethnic affiliation, such as the Michigan Election Survey. Despite assimilationist theories that predicted that forces such as diminished residential segregation and occupational specialization would lead to decreased importance of ethnicity in the lives of later-generation ethnics, these surveys show that a majority of later-generation individuals do indeed identify with an ethnic group in the surveys, and their ethnicity does seem to correlate with certain attitudes, behaviors, and voting patterns (Greeley 1971, 1974; Alba 1976; Abramson 1973).

In addition to these periodic national sample surveys, a new data source became available in the early 1980s. The U.S. census has only recently become a resource for research on *later*-generation whites. The decennial censuses through 1970 asked questions about the individual's birthplace and his or her parents' birthplaces. This made it possible to identify the first generation—immigrants themselves—and the second generation—the children of immigrants. (Together these two generations were known as the "foreign stock.") Yet the grandchildren and later descendants of immigrants were not identifiable in these censuses and were classified simply as "native white of native parentage." As the population of European origin progressed generationally, a smaller proportion of it consisted of "foreign stock" and a greater proportion disappeared into the category "native white of native parentage."

In the late 1970s leaders of organizations of white ethnic groups such as Irish-Americans, Italian-Americans, and Slavic-Americans pressured the government to change the census form by adding a question that would allow them to identify their potential members—the third and later generations. This move was resisted by the Bureau of the Census on the grounds that it would not produce "hard" enough data. In earlier tests of questions on ethnic identity, the Census Bureau's monthly Current Population Survey had found that ethnic identity was not very reliable—people changed their minds about it from survey to survey. However, at the last minute, responding to pressure from these ethnic organizations, the Census Bureau did add a question on ethnic ancestry (reproduced in Appendix A).[2]

---

2. The question appeared on the long form of the census that was sent to one out of every five households in the country. There was a blank line to record the ancestry of

The 1980 census asked people to describe their ancestry, allowing them to give up to three responses. For the first time, then, the ethnic ancestry of every individual was ascertained—not just that of the first and second generations. A total of 83 percent of Americans gave some ethnic response: a single ancestry was reported by 52 percent and multiple ancestry by 31 percent. The remaining 17 percent did not give a specific response about ancestry: 6 percent said American, 1 percent named a religious group or gave some other answer that was not codeable, and 10 percent gave no response at all (Bureau of the Census 1980a, 1–2).

These data provide valuable information for assessing the degree of assimilation and continued differences among white ethnics in later generations, making it possible to ascertain the degree of intermarriage, socioeconomic differences, and residential dispersion among white ethnics (Alba 1985a, 1985b; Lieberson and Waters 1985, 1988). The census data are an improvement over previously available sample survey data because the census allows identification of multiple ancestries. The census also provides coverage for the whole population—allowing analysis of ancestry data in small geographic areas.

However, there are various problems with both sample surveys and the 1980 census as *sole* sources of information on the ethnic identity of later-generation whites. Most important, the data reveal neither the strength nor the extent of ethnic identification. Presumably some of the people who answer that they are of a particular ethnic ancestry will attach a great deal of importance to that identity. For others, ethnicity is intermittently important, and still others will assume the label but little else. For example, it cannot mean the same thing for a fourth-generation Italian-American in a California suburb to say "I am Italian" as it does for a second-generation resident of Boston's North End, for whom chances in life, primary and secondary relationships, and so on are to a large extent bounded by the world of the ethnic group. These surveys affirm that individuals do maintain an ethnic identity, but cannot tell what this identity means to the individual, how and why people choose a particular ethnic identity from a

---

each person listed in the household. Multiple responses were accepted and the answer "American" was discouraged. The census coded two ancestries for each person who supplied two on the form and coded three ancestries for an individual if he or she was among the seventeen most common triple combinations reported to the census. For an in-depth analysis of these ancestry data for whites, see Lieberson and Waters 1988. Bean and Tienda 1987 discusses the results for people of Spanish origin, and Farley and Allen 1987 discusses the responses of blacks.

range of possible choices; how often and in what ways that ethnic identity is used in everyday life; and how ethnic identity is intergenerationally transferred within families.

In order to delve more deeply into these processes of ethnic identification for white Americans, I conducted in-depth interviews with sixty third- and fourth-generation white ethnics in suburban communities outside of San Jose, California, and Philadelphia, Pennsylvania, in 1986–87. These personal interviews provide an exploratory account of the nature and meaning of ethnicity for a population that has proved very elusive to in-depth analysis. Very little research has been done on the ethnicity of people who live in suburban areas that are not segregated by ethnic origin.[3] In fact, sociologists tend to equate suburbanization and residential integration with assimilation. Yet we know that later-generation suburban residents do continue to answer census or survey questions on ethnicity. Were respondents just inventing an answer to a census question when they said they were Irish-Italian, or did this identity have some meaning in their day-to-day lives?

The two suburbs I chose for the fieldwork were on opposite sides of the country. The first, a California suburb, was an area where a sociologist would least expect to find ethnicity. I tried to discover what kind of ethnicity exists when the structural forces that maintain it are not evident. Then a suburb outside of an older northeastern city—Philadelphia—was chosen, in part to see whether or not the same patterns held there as in California—whether somehow the ties of ethnicity would be stronger in the East, where the original immigrants from Europe first settled in great numbers. Since the general trend in the country has been toward increased mobility, higher educational achievement, and social mobility into the middle class for white ethnic groups, these middle-class suburbs could be seen as the cutting edge of the future development of white ethnicity. In fact, the respondents were at that very interesting point where they fall off the sociologist's map—having moved from urban neighborhoods that were previously ethnically defined, in many cases, to a suburb that was not ethnically defined.

The suburban areas were chosen specifically because they were not

---

3. See Fandetti and Gelfand 1983, di Leonardo 1984, and Martinelli 1983 for studies of Italian-Americans in suburban areas. Alba (1988, 1990) has conducted what I think is the first in-depth analysis of a randomly chosen sample survey focusing on later-generation ethnic identification. His survey examines the identification of Americans of single and mixed European origin in the Albany, N.Y., metropolitan area.

primarily populated by any one ethnic group.[4] Both areas are over-whelmingly white and upper-middle-class. The respondents were law-yers, engineers, managers, teachers, nurses, stockbrokers, and the like. Most were the first generation in their family to have profes-sional jobs. Most, but not all, were college-educated.

Although I deliberately added the Philadelphia sample after I had completed the interviews in California because I thought there might be some ways in which living in California dampened ethnic identity —through geographic mobility away from extended family ties and European immigrant communities, I actually found very few differ-ences between the two samples. The stories people told about family and ethnicity were very similar in these two suburban communities. Because the two samples were so very similar, I do not distinguish between them in the narrative that follows.

The samples were restricted to whites of European extraction and to Roman Catholics. The choice to interview only Americans of European origin was made because the theoretical question of interest was the meaning or lack of meaning of ethnicity to people in the last stages of assimilation—people for whom ethnicity is an option rather than an ascribed characteristic. As many sociologists have noted, racial identity as a non-white has had very different consequences for individuals in our society (Blauner 1972; Takaki 1987), and so I would expect that the processes and experiences I describe here would generally be different for that population.

The sample was drawn from Roman Catholics for three reasons. First, because I wanted to control for the effects of religion indepen-dently from those of ethnicity, I decided that comparing levels and content of ethnic identification within one religion would introduce fewer confounding factors than considering all religions at once. Second, the groups that experienced ethnic resurgence in the 1970s—Italians, Poles, and Irish—are mostly Roman Catholic. By interviewing Catholics the research would focus on a population that was the subject of much debate between the assimilationist and pluralist approaches to ethnicity (Alba 1976, 1044). Finally, I did not want to specify in advance which ethnic groups to interview because I was

4. The area of the California parish was approximately 80 percent white, 11 percent Asian, 7 percent Hispanic, and 2 percent black. The most common ancestries among whites were English, German, Irish, Italian, and Portuguese. The Philadelphia sample was chosen from an area that was 93 percent white, 5 percent black, 1.1 percent Asian, and .9 percent Hispanic. The most common ancestries among the whites there were German, Italian, Irish, English, Russian, and Polish.

particularly interested in people with mixed ethnic backgrounds and the process by which they either chose one of their ethnicities or chose not to identify with any ethnicity. By using a population of Catholics, I was sampling from among "potential ethnics," but was not pre-selecting any degree or kind of ethnic identification.

The question of whether the processes described here are different for other religious groups in the United States will ultimately have to be answered through further research with other samples. Jews may be more aware of and identified with their ethnic identity than the suburban Catholics I interviewed. Protestants may be further removed from their ethnic ancestries than Catholics owing to patterns of immigration to the United States, with northern and western Europeans coming before the more heavily Catholic central and southern Europeans. This would mean less ethnic identification overall for Protestants, and less societal sensitivity to that identification. Overall, then, one might assume that the patterns described here for Catholics will generally be true for other groups, but the intensity of feeling and attention to ethnicity will vary, depending on factors such as the degree to which religion overlaps with ancestry and the number of generations in the United States, which will vary by religion.

Using the "snowball" sampling technique, I started by interviewing active parishioners in the two suburbs chosen. At the conclusion of each interview, I asked if the respondent knew of another member of the parish who would be willing to be interviewed. If so, I then called the latter to set up an interview. Whenever possible, I also attempted to interview more than one generation in a family. Accordingly, I contacted the grown-up children of middle-aged respondents and the parents of younger respondents.[5]

The interviews were conducted in the respondents' homes and lasted between one and three hours. In addition to the formal interviews, I was invited to social events in both areas, including family gatherings, christenings, and holiday celebrations. These occasions provided opportunities for me to informally interview other extended family members and to observe family rituals and interactions.

Despite the restriction of the sample to white, suburban, middle-

---

5. I was not as successful as I would have liked in this endeavor, only interviewing two generations in six families—the Alberts, the Scottos, the Binets, the O'Keefes, the Williamses, and the Gilligans. In five other families I did not conduct in-depth interviews with more than one generation, but I did ask adult respondents about the ancestries of their children.

class Catholics, much of the diversity of ethnicity in America appeared in my sample. The majority of my respondents were of Irish, Italian, and Polish descent, but the final sample included people of Portuguese, Scottish, Welsh, English, German, French, Slovenian, Lithuanian, Serbian, Norwegian, Dutch, American Indian,[6] Spanish, Russian, and Czech origin. (Of course, some people had only a small fraction of one of these ethnicities present in their backgrounds.) The degree of intermarriage in the family backgrounds of the sample was relatively high—with only 40 percent of the sample describing only one ancestry in their backgrounds.

I began each interview with the census form and asked respondents how they would answer the ancestry question, reading them the instructions the Bureau of the Census provided. Next I asked the open-ended question, "Why did you answer in that way?" Then followed a series of questions about family history and ethnicity. The responses to those questions and further probing into the process of self-identification reveal some of the complicated mechanisms people use to shift and choose ethnic or ancestral affiliation. The interview schedule is reproduced in Appendix B, and a list of the respondents, along with information on their ancestry, occupation, age, residence, and education is presented in Appendix C. The names and all other identifying characteristics have been changed.[7]

These in-depth interviews, together with quantitative data on ethnic identification from the 1980 census, are used in the following chapters to explore the evolution and content of ethnic identity for later-generation whites in America. Sociologists have speculated about the extent of the persistence of ethnic identity beyond the third generation, and about the meaning of such identities for those involved. The 1980 census confirms that some degree of identity does persist, but only provides the beginning pieces of the puzzle of what this new or "symbolic" ethnicity entails. The interview material provides a rich exploratory account of the nature and meaning of ethnicity for this heretofore elusive population.

Chapter 2 describes two of the most important characteristics of

---

6. Although the sample was restricted to Americans of European origin, two individuals did describe some portion of Native American ancestry in their backgrounds.

7. In the process of changing the names for my respondents, I tried to make the new names reflect the ethnic connotations of the respondents' real names. Thus if a respondent had an Irish first name and an Italian last name, I gave them a similar pseudonym.

later-generation ethnicity in the United States: it involves choices and is dynamic. The influences on the choices people make about their own ethnic identity are discussed in chapter 3. Chapters 4 through 7 describe the content and meaning of ethnicity for the people interviewed. Chapter 4 explores the declining significance of the boundaries separating white ethnic groups in terms of socio-demographic phenomena such as intermarriage, socioeconomic discrimination, and residential segregation. Chapters 5 and 6 examine the cultural and social psychological significance that ethnic identity retains for the respondents. The last chapter discusses how the process and content of ethnic identification reinforce each other, and the implications and consequences ethnicity holds for this population and for society as a whole.

Flux and Choice
in American Ethnicity

Census and survey data on later-generation white ethnics in the 1970s and 1980s have yielded an interesting and what may appear at first to be a startling finding—ethnic identity is a social process that is in flux for some proportion of the population. Far from being an automatic labeling of a primordial characteristic, ethnic identification is, in fact, a dynamic and complex social phenomenon. The evidence for this comes from reinterview data that show changes in ethnic identity among individuals interviewed at two different points in time, age data that suggest changes in ethnic identification at particular points in the life cycle, and apparent simplifications in ethnic identity that occur when parents answer the census question for their children and when spouses answer for each other (Lieberson and Waters 1986).

The degree of intermarriage and geographic and social mobility among whites of European extraction in the United States means that they enjoy a great deal of choice and numerous options when it comes to ethnic identification. This population can increasingly choose how much and which parts of their ethnicity to make a part of their lives. Yet for the most part these options or choices are not recognized as such by the people who enjoy them.

The idea that ethnic self-identification is not biological or primordial and that it involves a great deal of choice may be startling to some people, because it is counterintuitive when viewed from the popular conception of ethnicity. The widely held societal definitions of race and ethnicity take the categories and classifications in place at any one time for granted, and hence do not generally see them as socially created or dynamic in nature. The common view among Americans is that ethnicity is primordial, a personal, inherited characteristic like hair color. Most people assume that ethnic groups are stable categories and that one is a member of a particular ethnic group because one's ancestors were members of that group. Thus one is French because one's ancestors were French and because the category French exists and has meaning. One may know that the Normans, the Franks, the Burgundians, and the Gauls were once separate groups who came to be known as French, but that does not necessarily make the category French any less "real" to a particular individual.

Yet most sociologists study ethnicity from social, situational, or rational points of view, seeking to understand the forces in society that create, shape, and sustain ethnic identity. They often defend such approaches from an opposite, biologically based understanding of ethnicity (Bonacich 1980; Patterson 1977; Bell 1975). Sociologists' definitions of ethnicity stress that it involves the *belief* on the part of people that they are descended from a common ancestor and that they are part of a larger grouping (see Weber [1921] 1968, 389; Shibutani and Kwan 1965, 47). The idea that membership in an ethnic group need not be hereditary, or directly related to a common lineage, is a direct challenge to this widely held view.

Recent theorizing by anthropologists and sociologists has focused on the cognitive, subjective, and perceptual notions of ethnicities. Frederik Barth (1969) shifted the focus of many anthropologists from defining and inventorying the cultural practices included in the definition of an ethnic group to examining the processes of constructing and maintaining ethnic boundaries. The critical features of ethnicity for Barth are the phenomena of self-ascription and ascription of others. This concern with the cognitive state of the actor has led to a wealth of studies of subjective ideas and perceptions as well as cultural meanings of ethnicity, social criteria for ascribing ethnic identities, the fluidity of ethnic boundaries, and varying combinations of ethnic and other social identities (Okamura 1981). Much of this research has been concerned with what Paden (1967) terms situational ethnicity—the particular social contexts and structures affecting an individual's invocation of one ethnic identity or another.

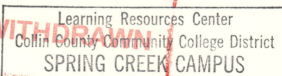

But the concern of Barth and others has been criticized as overly voluntaristic and subjective. As Jonathan Okamura points out, "The difficulty with this reasoning is obvious: it would appear to accord individuals the option to pursue whatever course of action they desire without consideration of the role constraints that may well proscribe such behavior" (1981, 458).

In fact, people's *belief* that racial or ethnic categories are biological, fixed attributes of individuals does have an influence on their ethnic identities. This popular understanding of ethnicity means that people behave as if it were an objective fact even when their own ethnicity is highly symbolic. This belief that ethnicity is biologically based acts as a constraint on the ethnic choices of some Americans, but there is nonetheless a range of latitude available in deciding how to identify oneself and whether to do so in ethnic terms. Whites enjoy a great deal of freedom in these choices; those defined in "racial" terms as non-whites much less.

Black Americans, for example, are highly socially constrained to identify as blacks, without other options available to them, even when they believe or know that their forebears included many non-blacks. Up until the mid twentieth century, many state governments had specific laws defining one as black if one-quarter or more of one's ancestry was black, or one out of four of one's grandparents were (Yetman 1985, 11). As late as the 1970s the Current Population Survey required its interviewers to determine the race of those they were interviewing "by observation." As a result some people were classified as "Negro" by the interviewer who did not classify themselves that way: 1.9 million out of a total of 22.9 million who were classified as "Negro" by the interviewer answered something else for themselves. Most answered "Don't Know" or "Other"; 126,000 said they were Spanish (Johnson 1974, 7). In any case, this shows how some groups may be socially constrained to accept an ethnic identity. The assumption by the official census takers was that others could determine the race of an individual on "objective," quasi-biological grounds without that person necessarily agreeing. There were no such assumptions or actual legal definitions governing choice of ancestry or identity for white Americans.

The fact that there are no longer any *legal* constraints on choice of ancestry does not mean these choices are completely "free" of social control. Certain ancestries take precedence over others in the societal rules on descent and ancestry reckoning. If one believes one is part

English and part German and identifies in a survey as German, one is not in danger of being accused of trying to "pass" as non-English and of being "redefined" English by the interviewer. But if one were part African and part German, one's self-identification as German would be highly suspect and probably not accepted if one "looked" black according to the prevailing social norms.

For white ethnics, however, ethnic identification involves *both* choice and constraint. Children learn both the basic facts of their family history and origins and the cultural content and practices associated with their ethnicity in their households. This process itself often involves a sifting and simplifying of various options.

One constructs an ethnic identification using knowledge about ancestries in one's background. Such information generally comes from family members and/or some type of formal documentation, such as a family Bible or a will. This information is selectively used in the social construction of ethnic identification within the prevailing historical, structural, and personal constraints. Often people know that their ancestors are from many different backgrounds, yet for one reason or another they identify with only some, or in some cases none, of their ancestors.

The interaction between choice and constraint in ethnic identification is most obvious in the case of the children of mixed marriages. But even the relationship between believed ethnic origin and self-identification for people of single ancestry involves a series of choices. For instance, individuals who believe their ancestry to be solidly the same in both parents' backgrounds can (and often do) choose to suppress that ancestry and self-identify as "American" or try to pass as having an ancestry they would like to have. The option of identifying as ethnic therefore exists for all white Americans, and further choice of *which* ethnicity to choose is available to some of them.

Furthermore, an individual's self-identification does not necessarily have to be the same at all times and places, although it can be. Someone whose mother is half Greek and half Polish and whose father is Welsh may self-identify as Greek to close friends and family and as Polish at work, or as Welsh on census documents. An individual may change ethnic identification over time, for various reasons. At various times and places, one is more or less at ease dropping or inventing a self-identification. In a local situation where everyone knows one's believed ethnic origins—for example, a small town where everyone knows your mother and father—it would be more difficult to self-identify exclusively with one or the other. If one moved to another locality this would probably become easier.

Data from the 1980 census and various sample surveys show the ways in which Americans exercise their ethnic options. These data address the question, if one has to choose just one ancestry from a mixed heritage, what rules govern the choice? Since ethnicity is rooted in common descent, there are strong expectations in our society that individuals will trace their ethnicity from their ancestors. There is actually an ambivalence and much confusion once this is attempted, however, because of the ways in which Americans reckon kinship. Americans believe that the mother and the father contribute equal amounts of genetic material to the child. Thus grandparents and great-grandparents on the father's side are just as related to the child as the ones on the mother's side. However, while Americans trace descent on both sides of their family tree, they also receive their surnames from the father's side, and women have generally taken their husband's name when they marry. This preference for the patrilineal line of descent has an enormous influence on the actual amount of knowledge people receive from their parents about their ancestors. This is especially true because of the importance of the surname in reckoning ethnic ancestry. Often someone who is uncertain about a person's ancestry will guess based on surname (I discuss this process in detail in chapter 3).

Although our social rules of kinship tell us that we should determine our descent by both maternal and paternal lines, and that all of our ancestors count equally, many surveys ask people for only one ethnic identity, and as we shall see from the interviews, in normal conversation people often mention only one or some of their ancestries when asked, "What are you?" Census and survey data do tend to support the hypothesis that people "reaffiliate" with one parent's ancestry, thus losing a part of their ancestral background. In general, people neither insist on naming all of their ancestries nor just call themselves American. Most pick and choose. And the trend is apparently toward more and more people making choices about their ethnic ancestry.[1]

1. Alba and Chamlin 1983 found that both later-generation and younger respondents to the NORC General Social Survey were more likely to respond that they had mixed ancestry; they also were more likely to identify with a single group than were earlier-generation and older respondents in the same situation. Thus younger and later-generation Americans were more likely to be faced with ambiguous ethnicity; yet they were more likely to deal with this by choosing one ethnic ancestry rather than by refusing

THE CHOICES ADULTS MAKE

The ways people come to an ethnic self-identification
in cases where an individual believes that his or her
different ancestries and must then make a decision
ancestry to identify with. Sometimes this is not even a
socialized so early in life that people are not even aware of it.

There are, however, quantitative data on how people choose between available ancestries: the National Election Study (NES) conducted by the University of Michigan asked respondents separately
for their ethnic ancestry and their ancestral birthplaces. Among
respondents to the study, 26 percent reported more than one ancestry for both of their parents and were able to choose a primary
identification for themselves, and another 10 percent reported more
than one ancestry for both of their parents but were unable to choose
a primary identification. A total of 36 percent of all respondents to
the survey thus reported more than one ancestry for both of their
parents.

Tom W. Smith (1981, 12) analyzed these responses to identify how
a respondent chose among the alternatives available. He reports that
of those who responded with one or more different nationalities for
their parents, 20.4 percent reported no identification for themselves,
5.9 percent chose a different ancestry from either of their parents,
14.5 percent selected an ethnicity shared by their parents, 26.4 percent chose their mother's ancestry and 35.8 percent chose their
father's ancestry. If one looks only at those who had to choose
between the different ancestries of their parents, 58 percent chose
their paternal ancestry and 42 percent chose maternal.

The Bureau of the Census's Content Reinterview Study is a second
source of quantitative data. In order to test the 1980 question on
ancestry, the Census Bureau reinterviewed a sample of individuals and
asked them a series of questions on parental, grandparental, and
ancestral birthplaces. It then compared the answers people gave with
those they had given to the census ancestry question. The Reinterview
Study provides some suggestive answers to the question of whether
individuals who believe their parents to be of mixed ancestry simplify

---

to choose. These authors conclude, based on these data, that a process of "reaffil-
iation" with one ethnic group is occurring. (Note that this also means that individuals
are choosing to "selectively forget" other possible ancestries in their past.)

all, and, if they do, whether they identify with the maternal or paternal line.[2]

The 1980 census ancestry question and the Michigan National Election Study are not strictly comparable. Yet the Census Bureau also found that people were more likely to choose the ancestries from their father's side of the family. Of those who chose an ancestry that matched their parents' or ancestors' birthplaces only on one side, 41 percent chose an ancestry that matched their maternal ancestors and 59 percent chose an ancestry that matched their paternal ancestors (Bureau of the Census 1986, p. 64). When faced with a heterogeneous group of ancestors, a person who is going to simplify or identify with one or the other side is slightly more likely to choose the father's ancestry, but obviously it is not an automatic process in which all individuals choose the paternal line to determine ancestry.

Even though it was a breakthrough for the 1980 census to allow more than one ancestry—and 31 percent of the population did list at least two—my interviews suggest that such surveys underestimate the mixing of the population. This is because it is often assumed when analyzing these surveys that *only* those giving a multiple ancestry are the result of ethnic intermixing. However, people frequently make choices and sift through their ancestries before naming an ancestry. Many people who give a multiple ancestry have simplified from an even greater number of possibilities, and many people who give a single ancestry are actually aware of multiple possible ancestries in their backgrounds.

CHOOSING AN ANCESTRY

In my interviews I explored the issue of how people decide how to answer a question about ethnic origin in a census or survey. I began each interview by showing people the census ancestry question and asking how they would answer it. Then I immediately asked the reason for that particular answer. The ways in which people described their family histories and the ways in which they came to their

2. The Census Bureau's Reinterview Study compared ancestry response with birthplace response for ancestors. The reader should interpret these data with some caution. Birthplace (or nativity) data and ancestry (or ethnic-origin) data are not always the same (Lieberson and Santi 1985). Armenians and Palestinians are scattered throughout the world, for instance, and family members are likely to have a variety of birthplaces, which would in themselves give no clue as to their descendants' ethnic origins.

answers reveal just how much sifting and sorting occurs *even before* they consider the question. The complex interplay among the different aspects of an individual's ethnic identification was an overriding theme in the interviews.

Very often over the course of an interview, individuals remembered an ancestry that was not even consciously a part of what they believed their ethnic origins to be. This selective forgetting is illustrated in the case of Laurie Jablonski, a 29-year-old social worker. Laurie reported at the beginning of the interview that she was fourth-generation Polish-German. Her great-grandparents on her mother's side had been German immigrants, her father's grandmother was German, and her father's grandfather was Polish. Laurie discussed at length the various elements that she thought made up her Polish and German heritage. Even though culturally her family observes many German customs and is very German-identified, Laurie often gives her ethnic identity simply as Polish when asked. She said this was because her last name was Polish, and that is often how others identify her. Thus though her self-identification in private and with her family is German-Polish, and she believes that her origin is more than three-quarters German, her self-identification to others is often only Polish.

However, a much more extreme example of simplification and "selective forgetting" became clear at the end of the interview. At the end of an hour-and-a-half interview, when the tape recorder was turned off, Laurie said that she had just remembered that she had some English in her too, that her grandmother had told her five years ago that one of her ancestors, she does not know which one, had been married to an English person. She recalled being really annoyed when her grandmother told her this and remembered thinking, "I am already this mishmash, don't tell me that I am anything else too."

Ted Jackson, a 27-year-old office worker, also reported feeling annoyance when he discovered that he really had more ancestral elements in his background than he had originally thought. He said he was of Irish, French, German, English, and Scottish ancestry: "I didn't even know I was Scottish until I got interested in my roots and I went over to my grandmother's. I didn't know I was English. I thought I was only a couple of things, but then she really made me feel like a dirt ball—throw everything else in there too."

Further probing in many of the interviews revealed ancestries in the histories of these people that were just deemed too inconsequential to mention. A respondent who seemed on the verge of forgetting an ancestry was Mike Gold, a 54-year-old lawyer, who reported that he would have answered English and French on the census form, and that he was fourth-generation American. When I asked why he would have answered English and French, he answered:

A: Well, my mother was English and my father was French and Polish.

Q: Then why would you not answer English, French, and Polish?

A: I don't know. I guess I just never think about the Polish.

The unimportance of certain ancestries to people is clear in the ways in which they naturally describe these ancestries as part of their origin immediately after giving themselves an ethnic label that does not include them. For instance, Bill Kerrigan, a 19-year-old college student:

Q: What is your answer to the census question?

A: I would have put Irish.

Q: Why would you have answered that?

A: Well, my dad's name is Kerrigan and my mom's name is O'Leary, and I do have some German in me, but if you figure it out, I am about 75 percent Irish, so I say I am Irish.

Q: You usually don't say German when people ask?

A: No, no, I never say I am German. My dad just likes being Irish... I don't know, I guess I just never think of myself as being German.

Q: So your dad's father is the one who immigrated?

A: Yes. On this side it is Irish for generations. And then my grandmother's name is Dubois, which is French, partly German, partly French, and then the rest of the family is all Irish. So it is only my maternal grandmother who messes up the line.

Thus in the course of a few questions Bill labeled himself Irish, admitted to being part German but not identifying with it, and then as an afterthought added that he was also part French. His identification as Irish was quite strong, both culturally and socially, which explains his strong self-labeling. Further in the interview, however, he described a strong German influence as he was growing up. His mother's first husband, who died before she married his father, had been a German immigrant, and he had spoken German with her. Bill's half brothers and sisters from that marriage were apparently quite German-identified, and Bill himself was quite knowledgeable about

his German maternal grandmother. He reported that his m
strongly committed to her German ancestry and would defini
mentioned it along with her Irish ancestry on the census fc
said he never thought of himself as German, however.

Another example is a 46-year-old manager, Rose Peters, who ᴄnose
between her Italian and Irish ancestries based on the ideas she got
about both from her parents:

Q: When you were growing up did you consider yourself ethnic?

A: Yes, I was very strongly Italian, because the Irish...whenever I was in
    a bad mood, that was the Irish in me. So I always related the Irish
    with the bad things and the Italian with all of the good things.

Q: Why?

A: I guess because every time I would do something bad, my mother
    would say, "Oh, that's those Irish eyes. That's the Irish from your
    father." The good things, like if I cleaned my room, she would say,
    "Oh, look, you are a Rosio," which was the Italian. So I thought all
    the Irish were hotheads and all the Italians had clean houses and
    good food.

People contradicted themselves frequently in the interviews because they had become so used to the simplifications of their ancestors' backgrounds that they did not even notice that their first answer
to the question was incomplete. Notice how Betty O'Keefe, a 60-year-
old housewife, did not even notice that she was telling me about a
French part to her ancestry:

Q: Ancestry?

A: Irish.

Q: Why?

A: Because the majority, the great majority, of my ancestors were Irish.

Q: Do you know anything about the immigrants?

A: It wasn't my father and it wasn't my grandfather. I met my great-
    grandmother, and she didn't have an Irish accent, so it must have
    been like in the 1840s with the famine Irish, I presume. That's my
    father's side. They have a branch that were French too, but mostly
    Irish.

There were many other cases in which other ancestries would "pop
up" in the course of an interview. And these "hidden ancestries" were
often present in people who had very strong identifications with only
those parts of their identities they "claimed" or recognized. Of

course, the selective identification described here is not just the choice of the individual. A large part of this simplification occurs when parents decide what they will tell their children about who they are and who their ancestors were.

THE LABELS GIVEN TO CHILDREN

Knowledge of one's ethnic ancestry is the result of sifting, simplifying, and distorting the knowledge one has about it in interaction with the labels others attach to it. Among the most influential of these labels are those given to children by their parents. We have just seen that the available survey data suggest that among people with a mixed back-ground who make a choice in a census or survey, there is a slight preference for the father's ancestry. The 1980 census data allow us to look closely at a small portion of the process of sifting that goes on before the individual begins to make his or her own decision.

In previous censuses and surveys, when one reported different ancestries for both parents on sample surveys, one was usually as-signed the paternal ethnicity by the interviewer on the assumption that ethnicity was transferred via the surname. For instance, the Current Population Survey did not ask parents to give an ethnic identity for their children in either 1972 or 1973. In both years the ethnic identity of a child was assigned by computer based on the responses of the parents. In 1972, children under the age of fourteen were allocated to ethnicities based on head-of-household information. Only in the event that the head of household's response was "Don't know" was the ancestry of the wife used to determine that of the child. In 1973 for the first time the ancestries of both parents were used to determine a child's ancestry, and if the parents had two separate ancestries, the child was allocated to the "Other" category containing all mixed-ancestry responses.[3] Thus until 1973 it was assumed that the ancestry of the child would always follow the paternal line and not the maternal line. As we have seen from the NES and CRS data, this process would misidentify approximately 40 percent of those who simplify their ancestry.

3. In 1973 if the head of the household and the wife were of differing origins, the child was put into the "Other" category for most combinations. However, if either the mother or father was of one of the Spanish-origin categories, the child was put into the appropriate Spanish category. There was a clear hierarchy of assignment here. Spanish origin took precedence over other origins.

The 1980 census did not follow this procedure, and so we are able to look at how parents label children. Since the census recorded an ancestry for everyone in the household and allowed for multiple ancestries for individuals, it is possible to examine the ancestry of children and relate it to that of their parents. Lieberson and Waters (1986) analyzed these responses. We reasoned that if a mother is of ancestry X and a father is of ancestry Y, a child should in theory be reported as XY, assuming that the parents' responses that they are X and Y are true and complete (an assumption that, as we have seen, is likely to be inaccurate in many cases).

As it turns out, a surprising number of children are *not* labeled as the exact combination of their parents' ancestries.[4] Table 1 presents the percentages of children correctly labeled by their parents where each parent is of a different ancestry. For example, when the father is of English ancestry and the mother of some other specified single ancestry, 57.7 percent of their children are fully and completely labeled as English plus the other ancestry. Overall between 40 percent and 70 percent of the children of such combinations are reported with labels that include both ancestries. Or, put another way, between 30 and 60 percent of the children are assigned something other than the logical combination of their parents' ancestries. Thus even in the case of Italian ancestry individuals who have the highest percentage of children labeled correctly, a sizeable number—almost 30 percent—are labeled something other than the logical combination of the two parents.

There are several possibilities for these "incorrectly" labeled children. One possibility is that they may just be called American, as commonly predicted by assimilationists who see intermarriage leading to a new hybrid American. This possibility is investigated in table 2, which shows the percentage of children labeled American according to the ancestry of their parents. The lowest percentage of children labeled American are in families where both parents share the same specified single ancestry. For instance, in families where both parents are of English ancestry, fewer than 1 percent of the children are described as American. In cases where both parents identify some

4. The analysis of the 1980 census data was restricted to American-born parents, both in their first marriage, with children living at home, under the age of eighteen, both parents present in the household, and no more children present in the household than the mother said she had borne. This should control for most children from previous marriages, adoptions, and the like.

TABLE 1

PERCENTAGE OF "CORRECTLY" LABELED CHILDREN IN
FAMILIES WHERE EACH PARENT WAS OF A DIFFERENT
SINGLE ANCESTRY, 1980

Ancestry	Father	Mother	Average
English	57.7	55.7	56.7
German	65.4	65.9	65.6
Irish	65.3	66.3	65.9
French	62.3	60.5	61.3
Italian	71.5	72.9	72.1
Scottish	63.9	57.7	61.1
Polish	68.1	72.3	70.2
Dutch	60.3	62.1	61.3
Swedish	61.9	64.7	63.4
Norwegian	63.9	64.1	64.0
Russian	57.5	54.3	55.9
Czech	66.7	64.4	65.6
Hungarian	62.3	61.9	62.1
Welsh	59.2	58.8	59.0
Danish	62.8	57.7	60.2
Portuguese	60.9	62.9	61.9
Mexican	41.3	46.6	43.9
Puerto Rican	37.9	43.4	40.1
Spanish	40.8	38.1	39.2
American Indian	45.5	49.1	47.0

SOURCE: Lieberson and Waters 1986, 86.

non-American ancestry for themselves, but do not share the same ancestry, a very small percentage of the children—between 3 and 5 percent—are labeled American. Thus, in the case of families where one of the parents is of English ancestry and the other parent is of some specified non-English, non-American ancestry, 3 percent of the children are labeled American. The only exception to this are families in which one of the parents is of Russian ancestry.[5]

In families where one parent specifies American ancestry only and

5. Russians and Hungarians show a very high percentage of children labeled American. When a Russian is married to an American, their children are called American a full 75 percent of the time, and when both parents are Russians, a relatively high proportion—18 percent—of their children too are labeled not Russian but American. More than likely Russians have such a high percentage of children labeled American because of the politics of the Soviet Union. If labeling oneself American is more of a political than an ethnic statement, then it would make sense in the current political environment for these people to label their children American. Hungarians may have a high percentage in this category for similar reasons.

TABLE 2

PERCENTAGE OF CHILDREN LABELED AMERICAN,
BY ANCESTRY OF PARENTS, 1980

Ancestry of Parent	Ancestry of Spouse		
	Same[a]	*American*	*Other*[b]
English	0.7	51.9	3.0
German	1.2	47.2	2.9
Irish	1.5	49.2	2.7
French	0.9	46.9	2.9
Italian	1.9	46.8	3.2
Scottish	3.3	56.8	4.3
Polish	2.6	59.5	4.9
Dutch	0.9	38.2	3.3
Swedish	1.4	49.3	2.9
Norwegian	0.7	57.5	2.9
Russian	18.4	75.4	15.9
Czech	2.2	52.5	4.6
Hungarian	13.0	65.3	8.3
Welsh	0.0	63.2	3.4
Danish	4.5	62.5	4.3
Portuguese	1.2	57.1	2.6
Mexican	0.0	34.1	1.7
Puerto Rican	0.5	42.8	3.8
Spanish	0.2	40.2	2.2
American Indian	1.0	47.5	5.3

SOURCE: Calculated from U.S. Bureau of the Census 1980b.
[a]Both parents share the same single ancestry—e.g., in the first row, both parents are of English ancestry.
[b]This parent specified a single ancestry that was different from the other parent's and not American.

the other parent names a specific single ancestry, one might expect a very large number of the children to be labeled American. After all, labeling the child American in this case would be giving it the same ancestry as one of its parents. In this situation many more parents do decide to label their children American as a response to the question of choosing between competing parental ancestries, but not all of them do so. In families where one parent gives English as his or her ancestry and the other gives American, 51.9 percent of the children are labeled American. In general, about 40 to 65 percent of children in families where parents do not share the same ancestry and one parent gives American as his or her ancestry are labeled American.[6] The exceptions to this general pattern are families where one of the parents is Russian or Hungarian.

Another possible reaction to the question of what ancestry to ascribe to your child is to give no response or say that you do not know or cannot decide. The census category "No Response" combines those who did not respond to the question and those who answered, "Don't know." The percentage of children with no response given for their ancestry is reported in table 3.

A comparison of table 2 with table 3 shows that the percentage of parents giving no response for their children is slightly higher on average than the numbers responding "American." Similarly, a lower percentage of parents give no response for their children when one of the parents is also "No Response" (column 3 of table 3) and one is of a single foreign ancestry than when one parent self-identifies as American and the other asserts a different single ancestry.

It does appear that it is more likely for parents who share the same single ancestry to answer "No Response" for their children rather than labeling them American. Where parents do not feel that any ancestry is a meaningful response for their children, or feel that ethnicity makes no difference for them, they thus do not for the most part turn to the label American. Rather, they tend simply to refuse to answer the question.

SIMPLIFICATION

In order to examine more closely exactly what happens to children who are not labeled correctly, the exact ancestry responses were analyzed for a small number of the largest ancestry groups. The results of this analysis are presented in table 4.

It is evident that the situation is very different depending on whether the parents are both of the same ancestry or of different ancestries. For example, where both parents are English, 93.8 percent of the children are also labeled English. Where one parent is English and the other is of another ancestry, the numbers answering with both ancestries fall to between 50 and 60 percent. Here we can see that

6. Of course, this analysis was limited to parents who were each of a different single ancestry. It is unclear whether parents who are themselves of mixed ancestry, and therefore more likely to have a more limited ethnic identification, may also be more likely to label their children American.

TABLE 3

PERCENTAGE OF CHILDREN LABELED
"NO RESPONSE," BY ANCESTRY OF PARENTS, 1980

Ancestry of Parent	Ancestry of Spouse		
	Same[a]	*No Response*	*Other*[b]
English	4.4	33.9	4.2
German	3.1	34.5	3.9
Irish	3.8	32.1	4.1
French	5.3	35.4	4.2
Italian	3.4	32.0	3.8
Scottish	4.0	41.9	4.7
Polish	3.3	30.0	3.7
Dutch	3.4	27.8	3.9
Swedish	2.1	35.7	4.1
Norwegian	4.4	35.1	3.7
Russian	5.1	43.7	4.7
Czech	3.4	47.0	3.9
Hungarian	3.6	42.3	4.1
Welsh	7.1	37.5	5.1
Danish	6.1	19.3	3.6
Portuguese	2.8	32.2	3.9
Mexican	3.9	34.4	3.3
Puerto Rican	4.6	38.5	4.6
Spanish	4.3	38.0	5.3
American Indian	4.2	33.9	4.8

SOURCE: Calculated from U.S. Bureau of the Census 1980b.
[a]Both parents share the same single ancestry—e.g., in the first row, both parents are of English ancestry.
[b]This parent specified a single ancestry that was different from the other parent's and not "no response."

parents who do not ascribe both ancestries to their children are giving them incomplete ethnic labels.

Some ancestries, such as Italian, do appear to be more popular ones to simplify to, and some, such as Scottish, appear to be very unpopular in certain combinations. But how much of this is owing to the appeal of the ancestry label and how much to other factors, such as whether it is the mother or the father who has the particular ancestry? Table 5 presents information on children who were not labeled with both parents' ancestries. The first column of table 5 gives the percentage of all of the children of those combinations who

TABLE 4

PARENTS, BY CHILDREN'S STATED ANCESTRY, 1980

Parents' Actual Ancestry	Exact Combination	Children's Stated Ancestry						
		English	German	Irish	Italian	Scottish	Unknown	American
English-English	93.8						4.4	0.7
English-German	60.9	14.7	14.4				4.5	2.9
English-Irish	55.0	19.9		16.0			4.6	2.6
English-Italian	61.2	10.5			15.4		5.2	4.2
English-Scottish	51.5	24.0				9.6	5.4	5.0
German-German	94.0						3.1	1.2
German-Irish	69.1		10.8	10.2			4.4	2.5
German-Italian	73.1		7.7		9.3		3.8	3.1
German-Scottish	67.6		11.8			10.5	2.2	3.9
Irish-Irish	92.4						3.8	1.5
Irish-Italian	77.7			6.1	7.7		3.2	3.7
Irish-Scottish	68.6			13.8		8.1	4.6	2.3
Italian-Italian	93.2						3.4	1.9
Italian-Scottish	72.5				11.8	3.9	3.9	2.6
Scottish-Scottish	88.2						3.9	3.3

SOURCE: Calculated from U.S. Bureau of the Census 1980b.

TABLE 5

SIMPLIFICATION OF CHILDREN'S ANCESTRIES, 1980

Parents' Ancestry	% Simplified	% Choosing Maternal Ancestry	% Choosing Paternal Ancestry
English-English			
English-German	29.1	39.1	60.9
English-Irish	35.9	36.8	63.1
English-Italian	25.9	33.9	66.0
English-Scottish	33.6	39.6	60.3
German-German			
German-Irish	21.0	33.4	66.6
German-Italian	17.0	23.1	77.0
German-Scottish	22.3	24.8	75.2
Irish-Irish			
Irish-Scottish	21.9	24.6	75.4
Italian-Italian			
Italian-Scottish	15.7	25.0	75.0
Scottish-Scottish			

SOURCE: Calculated from U.S. Bureau of the Census 1980b.

simplified their ancestry and the second and third columns show the percentages who chose their mother's ancestry or their father's ancestry. The table shows that in all cases there is a preference for the father's ancestry. Between 60 and 77 percent of those simplifying choose to simplify to the father's as opposed to the mother's ancestry.

RELATIVE POPULARITY OF THE GROUPS

Given this preference for the father's ancestry, then, does the labeling of children by parents in mixed marriages tell us anything about the relative popularity of the various ethnic groups? In other words, given that a certain bias exists toward choosing the father's ancestry, if one controls for that bias, which ancestries are most popular?

Table 6 presents the percentages of children whose ancestries were simplified who were assigned their father's ancestry. It is clear that the preference for the father's ancestry was not uniform across ancestries. For instance, in the case where the mother was English and the father Scottish, only 38 percent of the children were labeled Scottish. However, in the case where the mother was of Scottish descent and the father of English, a full 80 percent of the simplifiers were assigned

TABLE 6

PERCENTAGE OF CHILDREN WHOSE ANCESTRY WAS
SIMPLIFIED TO PATERNAL ANCESTRY, 1980

Father's Ancestry	Mother's Ancestry					
	English	*German*	*Irish*	*Italian*	*Scottish*	*Mean*
English		63	69	58	80	68
German	60		66	73	76	69
Irish	58	67		65	88	69
Italian	72	80	72		100	81
Scottish	38	74	63	50		56
Mean	57	71	67	61	86	

SOURCE: Calculated from Bureau of the Census 1980b.

their father's ancestry. Once again, Italian appears to be a strong ethnicity and Scottish appears to be unpopular.

Another way of examining preferences of ancestry while controlling for the preference for the father's ancestry is to examine the ratio of choice of ancestry. In the situation where both parents' ancestries have an equal influence on the ancestry of the child, the ratio in the following equation should equal 1. That is, the ratio of those choosing ancestry A when the father is A to those choosing ancestry B when the mother is B should be equal to the ratio of those choosing ancestry B when the father is B to those choosing ancestry A when the mother is A. If the ratios are not equal to 1 that means that, even after controlling for the general preference for father's ancestry over mother's, the relative pull of the ancestries involved is affecting the choice of ancestry made by these parents for their children. In equation form:

$$\frac{\text{father A/mother B}}{\text{father B/mother A}} = 1 \quad \text{when A and B are equally popular ancestries}$$

These ratios are presented in table 7. In the pairwise comparisons it is clear that some ancestries are chosen far more often than others, even when controlling for the preference for the father's ancestry. In the case of the pairing of the two extremes—the popular Italians and unpopular Scottish—the inequality between the two is quite striking. In the case of the Germans and the Irish, on the other hand, the ancestries seem to have an equal pull and the ratio is equal to 1. Ranking these ancestries according to their relative use in this simplification process leads to the following order:

1. Italian
2. English
3. Irish
4. German
5. Scottish

We can only get such rankings for this small number of ancestries because the underlying *N*'s become too small, but we can nonetheless use these rankings to begin to address the question of the kinds of choices people are making about ancestries and what that has to tell us about the state of ethnicity in the United States today. If, as Lieberson (1985, 447) suggests, a question on ancestry "approximates for some respondents a sociological equivalent of an ink blot test," the results of these analyses suggest something about the perceptions

TABLE 7

ANCESTRY CHOICES FOR CHILDREN,
CONTROLLING FOR PARENTAL INFLUENCE, 1980

Ancestry A	Ancestry B	Parental Choice Ratios[a]
English	German	1.13
English	Irish	1.63
English	Italian	0.496
English	Scottish	6.18
German	Irish	1.0
German	Italian	0.45
German	Scottish	1.0
Irish	Italian	0.8
Irish	Scottish	4.48
Italian	Scottish	1,200.0

SOURCE: Calculated from U.S. Bureau of the Census 1980b.
[a]Parental choice ratios are the ratio of those children labeled with ancestry A when father is A to those labeled with ancestry B when mother is B over the children labeled with ancestry B when father is B to those labeled with ancestry A when mother is A. The ratio is equal to 1 when both ancestors are equally popular choices, for example, German and Irish. The ratio is greater than 1 when ancestry A is the more popular, e.g., the popular Italians paired with the unpopular Scots. It is smaller than 1 when ancestry B is the more popular.

people have of ethnicity in the United States today. I shall explore these issues in depth when I examine the images people currently hold of various ancestries. But these quantitative data suggest the same conclusions the interview data point to. When given a choice among European ancestries, the more recent, more "ethnic" of the groups are chosen. In other words, the more "ethnic" the group, the more desirable as an identity choice.

CHANGES ASSOCIATED WITH AGE

The 1980 ancestry data also allow an examination of changes in ethnic identity within one generation—that is, changes in people's ethnic identities at different ages and between surveys. These data show that a portion of the population simplify or change their ancestry responses in their own lifetimes, a finding that challenges one of our commonly held beliefs about ethnicity—that it is a physical or permanent aspect of oneself. Data from censuses and surveys and my interview material show that some people do indeed change their ethnic identities—or at least their reports of their ethnic identities at particular points in the life cycle.

Reinterview studies demonstrate that the decisions some individuals of mixed ancestry make about which ethnicity to identify with change frequently. The changes documented in these reinterview studies dramatically illustrate the fluidity that characterizes ethnic identification for one portion of the white ethnic population. In the early 1970s the Bureau of the Census's Current Population Survey, an interview conducted in the respondent's home, included a question on ethnic ancestry for the first time. It was a closed-ended question, forcing the respondent to choose a single ancestry from among thirteen choices, among them "Other" and "Don't Know." If respondents gave more than one ancestry, interviewers were directed to put them into the "Other" category. In 1971, 1972, and 1973, respondents were matched and reinterviewed and their responses on ethnic origin at two different points in time were compared. Both the initial interview and the reinterview were conducted by trained interviewers.

Overall, the consistency rate between years was quite low. In less than 65 percent of the cases was the same response obtained one year later. The rate of consistency varied, however, with 80–95 percent of Poles, Cubans, Italians, Mexicans, blacks, and Puerto Ricans giving consistent responses, but only 50 percent of those originally responding English, Scottish, and Welsh providing the same response a year later (Johnson 1974, 1). Table 8 gives the percentages reporting the same origin in 1972 as in 1971 and the percentages of those groups of first- and second-generation foreign stock. The groups with the lowest consistency in response are those whose peak immigration years were the longest ago—the northwestern Europeans who have been in the United States the longest. Groups that have arrived relatively recently, such as Italians, are more likely to contain immigrants or children of immigrants than groups such as the English, who came much earlier. The newer groups thus have a much higher consistency rate, such as 87.8 percent for Italians. The other groups with high consistency rates are minority groups such as blacks and Mexicans. In fact, the CPS report found that the consistency of reporting of ethnic origin did not vary with basic demographic and social characteristics such as sex or education. The distribution of the population among the various groups was also not affected by this inconsistency—approximately the same percentages shifted into and out of these various categories. The only factor that seemed to explain the level of inconsistency, the report concluded, was the specific group of origin itself (Johnson 1974, 7).

The pattern in the choices made by people switching ethnicities suggests that many of them are people who have multiple ancestries in their backgrounds who identify with one ancestry at one point but give more detailed responses listing more than one ancestry at another point. The responses for 1971 and 1972 are cross-tabulated in table 9 to show the answers given by those people who did not give the same response in 1972 as in 1971. A large percentage of those who in 1971 gave an "older" ancestry such as German, Irish, or English chose the category "Other," which included multiple ancestries, in 1972. Thus the Current Population Survey reinterviews suggest that for some later-generation white Americans, the choice of ancestry made for a survey like this is quite labile. This is consistent with the flux we saw in the process of parents labeling children.

A reinterview process was also conducted by the NORC General Social Survey, which again showed that for a segment of the population ethnic ancestry response changes over the years. In a reinterview in 1974 of those interviewed in 1973, only 74 percent consistently defined their ethnicity or lack of ethnicity in both years.[7] This

---

7. This is higher than the Current Population Survey reinterview probably because the General Social Survey provided more choices of ancestries for the respondent.

TABLE 8

CONSISTENCY OF ETHNIC RESPONSE, 1971 AND 1972

Ethnic Ancestry	Percentage Reporting the Same Origin in 1972 as in 1971	Foreign Stock as Percentage of Origin, 1970
Puerto Rican	96.5	90.8
Negro	94.2	
Mexican	88.3	44.5
Italian	87.8	48.4
Cuban	83.3	89.1
Polish	79.2	46.5
Spanish	78.9	57.1
German	66.1	14.2
Other (includes multiple ancestries)	62.5	
Russian	62.3	88.8
French	62.1	6.3
Irish	57.1	8.8
English, Scottish, Welsh	55.1	8.3
Don't know	34.9	
All groups	64.7	

Source: Johnson 1974, table A, p. 1; table B, p. 3.

response consistency rate can be compared with the rate on other questions asked by the GSS; for instance, 97 percent of respondents were consistent on region of residence at the age of sixteen, 92 percent on religious preference, and 85 percent on father's education (Smith 1980, 14).

The Bureau of the Census also did a reinterview check of responses to the ancestry question in 1980. Unfortunately, however, its Content Reinterview Study is not directly comparable to the CPS and GSS reinterview studies.[8] Yet despite all of the serious differences between the census and the interview questions, the Census Bureau did calcu-

8. This is because the CPS and the GSS did a reliability check by asking people the same question at two points in time and matching the results. The Content Reinterview Study seems to have aimed rather at checking the validity of the ancestry response. Interviewers did not ask the same ancestry question of people they reinterviewed. Rather, they asked a series of probing questions to more or less expose how people traced their ancestry. The census ancestry question reproduced in Appendix A asked simply for ancestry. The Content Reinterview Study asked a series of questions on the respondent's birthplace, the birthplaces of the respondent's parents and grandparents,

late the matched ancestries for many of the large ancestry groups. In a finding consistent with that of the CPS reinterview study, the census found that it was the groups of older northwestern European ancestry —English, German, Irish, and Scottish—that had lower consistency responses. In many reinterviews people changed their response from one of these older groups to American. These major surveys all point to the fact that some people are not claiming the same ancestry every year. Interviewed in 1971, an individual might be English; interviewed in 1972, he or she might be German. Some proportion of whites whose ancestors came more than two generations ago change their minds about what ethnic label to claim about as readily as they change their minds about presidential candidates or social issues.

AGE DATA

Another way to measure changes in ethnic identification over time is through an analysis of age by ethnic identification. The ideal data for this question would be a longitudinal study in which the researcher asked the respondent at 18, and then again at 19, at 20, and so on, about his or her ethnic ancestry, to see if any changes occur at particular ages. However, longitudinal data of this type are not available. In the absence of such repeated individual surveys, researchers have examined patterns in age data by years, thus inferring longitudinal changes from cross-sectional data. (Lieberson and Waters 1986; Smith 1983; Alba and Chamlin 1983).

The percentage of people reporting a single ancestry as opposed to multiple ancestry also changes at various ages. There is a definite

---

and "earlier generations on your mother's side and earlier generations on your father's side." If all of the responses to these questions indicated the United States or were "Don't Know," the respondent was asked, "In what country were your ancestors who first came to the United States born?" If more than one country was given, a further question was asked, forcing the respondent to choose a single country: "Which one of the countries you reported best describes your ancestry?" The Content Reinterview Study thus cannot really be used to check the consistency of the ancestry response because of its very different line of questioning. In the very important case of those who reported multiple ancestry on the 1980 census form, the Reinterview Study cannot be used to ascertain whether they continued to report the same level of complexity or continued to make the same choice about which ancestry to name as their primary one at another point in time. A detailed coding procedure was devised for the Content Reinterview Study to match birthplace responses to ancestry responses. In effect, if a person of multiple ancestry reported any forebears born into any of his or her ancestry-response nationalities, a match, or consistent response, was coded.

TABLE 9

ETHNIC ORIGIN AS REPORTED IN MARCH 1971 AND MARCH 1972
(Current Population Survey)

Ethnic Origin Reported in March 1972

Ethnic Origin Reported in March 1971	German	Italian	Irish	French	Polish	Russian	English	Spanish	Negro	Other	Don't Know	Not Reported
German	66.1	.1	2.1	.7	.4	.3	5.6	.1	.1	20.8	1.9	1.9
Italian	.6	87.8	1.2	.5	.3	.0	.5	.4	.0	6.8	.2	1.7
Irish	3.8	1.0	57.1	.5	.2	.0	11.4	.1	.0	17.3	6.5	2.2
French	2.5	.1	2.2	62.1	1.1	.1	7.3	.5	.0	21.0	.7	2.3
Polish	1.0	.3	.3	.5	79.2	1.4	1.4	.0	.0	13.2	.2	2.2
Russian	1.1	.5	.4	.5	3.6	62.3	.5	.0	.0	25.9	1.2	3.5
English	4.7	.4	6.9	1.4	.2	.0	55.1	.1	.3	23.1	5.1	2.4
Spanish	.5	.3	.2	.5	.0	.0	1.7	88.1	.5	4.1	.1	3.8
Negro	.0	.0	.0	.0	.0	.0	.0	.0	94.2	1.6	.4	3.7
Other	8.3	1.0	5.2	1.9	1.1	.8	10.3	.3	.9	62.5	4.0	3.6
Don't know	6.6	.4	6.7	1.5	.1	.2	19.7	.0	.9	26.5	34.9	2.6
Not reported	6.7	3.8	4.8	.6	2.4	1.3	11.2	1.0	8.9	29.4	6.4	23.3

SOURCE: Johnson 1974, table E, p. 5.

pattern in age changes in the level of detail of ethnic reporting. Lieberson and Waters (1986) report that among third-generation respondents to the 1979 Current Population Survey, the percentage giving a single-ancestry as opposed to a multiple-ancestry response is trendless up through ages 15–19. However, there is a sharp jump from 40 percent single ancestry in that group to 50 percent single ancestry at ages 20–24. There is also a sharp decline between these two age groups in the number reporting themselves as having a triple ancestry, from 6.4 to 4.0 percent. We concluded that these changes in the level of complexity of ancestry reporting are simplifications that occur at the age of separation of young adults from their parents' homes. At this point—between 15 and 24—young adults simplify their ancestries by identifying with only one or two of their possible ancestries.[9]

A further analysis of the 1979 Current Population Survey data provides more support for this hypothesis. Table 10 shows the changes in the living arrangements of third-generation young white adults through these years. The changes in level of complexity of ancestry reporting do coincide with changes in the living arrangements of these young people. At ages 15–19, only 9.8 percent were living on their own or in their own new families. However, by ages 20–24, a majority of over 60 percent were, and by ages 25–29 almost 89 percent were living away from their parents. As these young adults form new families, it is most likely that they start reporting their ancestry for themselves rather than having it reported for them by their parents—who might be more likely to give a greater level of detail.

Table 11 cross-tabulates ancestry by age and domicile for third-generation and later non-blacks. Young adults living on their own had a consistently higher percentage of single-ancestry responses regardless of age. For instance, among those aged 20–24 who were still living with relatives, 31.6 percent reported a single ancestry, while 51.7 percent of those living on their own or with a spouse reported a single ancestry. The number of triple-ancestry responses was also dramatically higher among those living at home with their parents (7.3 percent for those aged 20–24 living at home, as opposed to 2.8

---

9. It is assumed that parents will give more detailed reports on their children's ancestry than the children themselves do. The parents will combine the mother's and the father's ancestries to label their children. Elsewhere I assume that in general *self*-reporting of ethnic ancestry will yield more information than other reporting. In that light, the case of reporting of children's ancestry is the exception to the rule.

TABLE 10

DOMICILE OF
THIRD-GENERATION NON-BLACKS, BY AGE, 1979

Age	Living with Relatives[a]	Independent[b]
15–19	90.2	9.8
20–24	39.2	60.8
25–29	11.3	88.7

SOURCE: U.S. Bureau of the Census 1979a.
[a]Includes other relatives (including children) of heads of house-holds, non-relatives of heads of households living with relatives, and non-relatives of heads of households with no relatives of their own.
[b]Includes heads of households, wives of heads of households, and non-relatives living together.

TABLE 11

ANCESTRY RESPONSE OF THIRD-GENERATION AND LATER
NON-BLACKS, BY AGE AND DOMICILE, 1979 (%)

Age	Single Ancestry	Double Ancestry	Triple Ancestry	No Response
Independent				
15–19	48.6	35.3	2.2	13.9
20–24	51.7	34.5	2.8	11.0
25–29	50.0	38.0	2.7	10.3
Living at Home				
15–19	29.6	55.0	8.0	7.4
20–24	31.6	54.6	7.3	6.5
25–29	37.4	50.2	5.6	6.8

SOURCE: U.S. Bureau of the Census 1979a.

percent for those living on their own). Finally, the percentage of young adults unable or unwilling to give an ancestry response was much higher among those living away from their parents.

Findings from the 1980 census mirror those of the 1979 CPS. Because of the much larger sample available from the 1980 census, it is possible to look at the cross-tabulation of age by ancestry for single

TABLE 12

REPORTING OF ANCESTRY, BY AGE, 1980

Age	% Single Ancestry	% Mixed Ancestry	N (in hundreds)
15	61.4	38.6	40,550
16	61.6	38.4	41,709
17	61.9	38.1	42,615
18	63.0	37.0	42,414
19	65.0	35.0	43,741
20	66.0	34.0	43,331
21	67.0	33.0	42,465
22	67.4	32.6	42,148
23	67.8	32.2	41,840
24	68.4	31.6	41,005
25	68.6	31.4	40,991
26	67.6	32.4	39,538
27	68.2	31.8	39,177
28	68.0	32.0	36,963
29	68.1	31.9	37,628
30	68.8	31.2	37,284

SOURCE: Calculated from U.S. Bureau of the Census 1980b.

years of age.[10] The cross-tabulation of age by level of complexity of ancestry reporting is presented in table 12 for ages 15 through 30.

By looking at single years of age, we can see exactly when these changes begin to occur. The percentage reporting a single ancestry as opposed to multiple ancestry is quite steady through age 17; however between ages 17 and 21, it increases by about 6 percent, and then gradually hovers between 68 and 69 percent through age 30. Thus in the years between 17 and 21, when many young people leave home for college or the military, or marry and form their own homes, a portion of them also tend to simplify their ethnic identification.

Smith (1983, 20–21) reports a similar finding from the General Social Survey ethnic data. He reports that the GSS shows parental informants mentioning both ancestries for the children of ethnically mixed marriages. Yet the number of single ancestries rises with age after the teen years. He attributes the rise in proportions with a single ancestry after age 25 to real differences among cohorts in the proba-

10. These data are not directly comparable to the 1979 CPS data because they are for the second generation and beyond.

bility of being the product of single-ancestry parents. However, he attributes the sharp increase in single ancestry in the late teens and early adulthood to the shifts that occur when respondents report their own ancestry rather than having it reported for them by their parents. Apparently, parents will label a child with both ancestries, but the young adult simplifies their response to a single ancestry.[11] The age data suggest that a portion of the population that would have had a multiple ancestry reported for them by their parents, report a single ancestry for themselves once they begin reporting for themselves. The process of simplification can thus be seen to occur for an ever-increasing proportion of the population as they proceed through their lives.

There is also evidence from the interviews of people changing their ancestries, or at least becoming more aware of or involved with their ancestries at certain points in their lives. Most of my respondents by far reported that the time when they became very aware of their ethnicity was at the beginning of young adulthood. This is consistent with patterns in the census and survey data suggesting that this is a time at which flux occurs in ethnic identification. When asked about times when they became especially aware of their own and others' ethnicities, most people mentioned the transition from living at home with their parents to being independent. For many who had grown up in ethnically homogeneous environments, leaving home was the first time they were exposed to people from other ethnic groups. For many older men this occurred during military service. The experience of Tom Scotto, a 60-year-old small business owner, is typical:

> When you are a kid you don't think of yourself as anything. Sure, I knew I was Italian, but a lot of other people were too. It seems that everyone was Italian. It was just natural to be Italian. It was not until I left the neighborhood and went into the Navy that I started being really aware of it. Then when I would meet guys in the Navy, I would sort of seek out the other Italians. You had something in common with them. You would say, well, "He's an Italian from Brooklyn," or, "He is an Italian from so and so." I would also get ribbed by the other guys about being Italian, just good-natured. No one would dare say anything bad to my face.

For Paul Binet, a 57-year-old Protestant engineer from the South of English, Scottish, and Welsh descent, ethnicity when he was growing

---

11. This is consistent with Alba and Chamlin's findings, on analysis of the same GSS data, of a marked increase among younger cohorts in the odds that individuals with mixed or ambiguous ancestries will identify with a single group (Alba and Chamlin 1983, 246).

up meant being white. Aside from the differences between blacks and whites that he was quite aware of as a child, he does not recall any ethnic consciousness at all. However, when he joined the Army he realized that for others ethnicity could be quite important:

> When I was in the service, the company I went to boot camp with had about sixty guys and about forty out of the sixty were French, Cajun from Louisiana. They spoke mostly French. A very distinctive group. That is probably the only time I have ever been exposed to that. The only time I have ever been with a fairly significantly ethnic group.

For the younger people I interviewed, it was not military service that brought them into contact with different kinds of people, but the experience of going away to college. Joyce Hoffman, a 36-year-old teacher, did not realize that other people were more "truly" German than her family until she went away to college "and met people who really were ethnic." Other respondents reported that when people got to know each other in college dormitories, the conversation would often work its way around to comparing ethnicities.

The theme that characterizes many of these descriptions is that it is through meeting someone different from themselves that people's own ethnicity becomes clearer. By contrasting their own approaches to life, values, food, and personality to those of others from different backgrounds, these young people became aware that their ethnic backgrounds had the effect of making them different from others, and sometimes similar to those from the same ethnic group. This experience is often compounded by the fact that going away to college also sometimes involves moving to a different location, where, in addition to the people you meet in school, there are different people living all around you. For instance, Patrick O'Connor, a 26-year-old student, began to realize that he felt very Irish as a result of being around Italians:

> I was aware that I was Irish when I was a kid and that it might mean something, but I was not aware of what it meant and it was just a name. But when I moved to the city to go to school, it was different. I noticed more well-defined ethnic groups in the city. And I had a roommate who was a hard-core Italian from Brooklyn. It was very clear. The differences were very clear. Then I went to Italy for a semester and became much more aware of the different kinds of Catholicism, and it began to assume more of a shape and I could see that there were a lot of really Irish things in my background that I had not identified as Irish.

The other points in the life cycle mentioned by respondents as affecting their awareness and degree of ethnic identity include the time when young couples first have children. Many respondents mentioned that at this point they discussed what they would tell their children about their ethnic backgrounds, even when they had not been concerned with the subject before.

Finally, some have suggested that ethnic identity again becomes a salient issue for older people (Hoyt and Babchuk 1981; Johnson 1985). The argument is that ethnicity provides an integrative mechanism to counteract some of the alienation associated with aging (Hoyt and Babchuk 1981, 77). One respondent, who was just sixty at the time of the interview, seemed to suggest that his ethnic identity was increasing in importance as he got older. Tom Scotto says:

> Now definitely as I get older, it gets more important. It is important to have a sense of identity as you get older. To know who you are. You realize as you get older what is important to you. You do not understand this yet because you are still young. But you can't get older without learning some things. And it just gets more important to know who you are and what your roots are as you get older.

WHO ANSWERS THE CENSUS OR SURVEY

The changes in ethnic identification that show up in these reinterview studies and the age changes may reflect actual flux in ethnic identification over the life courses of individuals. However, a portion of these changes may also be owing to the design of the survey or census itself. For instance, the age changes just described are actually an interesting case of intergenerational and life-span changes being intertwined. Since the head of the household answers the CPS questions, the ancestry responses for children up through the age when they leave home (18–25) are actually labeling by their parents, not self-identification. So, rather than strictly measuring changes in self-identification over time, these age changes are tracking evolution from identification by a parent to self-identification by young adults.

Another example of seeming changes in self-identification, this time in the reverse direction—changes from self-identification to other-identification—occurs in the ethnic identification of married women. Lieberson and Waters (1986) found differences in the level of reporting of detail of ancestry between married and unmarried women in an analysis of 1980 census data. In general, we found that married women were more likely to be reported as being of unmixed ancestry than unmarried women. We speculated that this might be because of the census enumeration procedure. It is possible that husbands were filling out the census form and knew or just reported less detail about their wives' ancestry than the latter might have. Unmarried women who answered the form themselves reported a greater degree of detail about their own ethnic ancestry. This hypothesis is consistent with findings from the GSS, noted by Tom W. Smith, that reports of spouse's ethnicity are indeed less detailed and sparser than are the subject's self-reported ethnicity (Lieberson and Waters 1986, 89).

In addition to this enumeration issue, Lieberson and Waters (1986) reported that women with a single ancestry were likely to be married to men with a single ancestry, and that this varied by educational level, leading us to conclude that "among women with less education, there is a specially strong tendency to distort and simplify in order to match up with the spouse in a common ethnic ancestry" (p. 14).

In both of these cases, marriage per se thus seems to cause changes in women's ethnic identification. In one case, the possibility exists that these census reports of ancestry are actually not changes in how the women would identify themselves. Rather, they are simplifications in ancestry reporting stemming from the fact that someone else, presumably the husband, filled out the census form. In the other case, there seems to be a possibility that the women themselves might distort their own ethnic identification in order to stress particular parts of their ancestry to "match up" with their husband's ancestry.[12]

In my interviews with families, I did find evidence that parents would not necessarily give the same ancestry answer for their children that the children themselves would give. This would explain some of the changes at the age of separation that are so evident in the census

12. The presumption of Lieberson and Waters 1986 that the husband may have filled out the census form, and that this may account for some of the differences in level of complexity reported for married versus unmarried women, is a plausible one. Unfortunately, the census PUMS data file is such that one cannot identify who in the household filled out the census form. The possibility that some people in a household may know less about the ancestry of others, or may give a different answer than the latter themselves would, is recognized by some researchers. In fact, the Current Population Survey reinterview may have had such a low consistency rate because different individuals may have answered the questions for the reinterview and for the original interview. In the Current Population Survey, women were most likely to be answering the questions, because they were more likely to be at home when the interviewer called. In a 1970 Current Population Survey check on this issue, it was found that "75% of the women of voting age reported for themselves as compared with 34% of the men" (Bureau of the Census 1970, p. 7). So some of the changes in reporting of ethnicity between the years in the CPS reinterview study could be owing to changes in the respondent from year to year.

and survey data. For the most part among the population I interviewed, however, rather than the children themselves wanting to
simplify when they were eighteen, it would appear that the parents
underestimated the youngsters' attachment to their ethnicity.[13]

For instance, some parents who could give detailed ethnic ancestries for themselves were sure that their children did not think of
themselves in ethnic terms. Anne Gold, a 52-year-old X-ray techni-
cian, thought of putting American down for her children—yet mo-
ments later she recognized that her son would not label himself
American:

> Q: What would you put for your children's ancestry?
>
> A: Oh, my gosh, I would just have to say "American," because otherwise
>   it would just go on forever.
>
> Q: What do you think they would answer for themselves?
>
> A: American, I think.
>
> Q: Do they know that their ancestors were English and Irish?
>
> A: Yes, they do.
>
> Q: Do they ever ask about it?
>
> A: Well, yes, the oldest one is really into having a lot of Irish in his
>   background. He thinks it is really cool.
>
> Q: So do you think that maybe he might have answered "Irish"?
>
> A: Yes, well, he just might have. He loves being Irish.

Rose Peters also thought she would label her children American,
because her own ancestry seems so complicated:

> Q: So are you anything else besides Irish, Italian, Welsh, and
>   Lithuanian?
>
> A: There's bits. Like there is bits of French. There is bits of German. A
>   little of everything, I think. Now I tell my kids, they say, "What am
>   I?" and I say, "You are American." Because I figure we are a mixture
>   of it all, and that is what they are.

The differing responses of the mother, father, and children in the
Richter, Kerrigan, and Albert families indicate that family members
have very different ideas about the amount of knowledge and interest
other members have in their ancestry. This varying interest and

---

13. I do not know how to reconcile this inconsistency. I found evidence of both
simplification and more complexity in the responses of young adults.

knowledge would lead to different answers in surveys or changes in the answers depending on who was answering for the family.

I asked Ben and Barbara Richter what their ten children would put on the census form if they were answering for themselves. Ben Richter, a 56-year-old retired telephone company manager, is fourth-generation French, German, and Irish, and Barbara Richter, a 51-year-old housewife, is third-generation Irish. Barbara Richter was not sure that the children were even interested in whether or not they were Irish, except for one daughter:

Q: What do you think they would answer on the census form?
A: I do not know really. I do not think they think about whether they are Irish or not. The boys especially. I do not think you would get a whole lot out of them on that. Kathy probably would answer something. She is one of the older girls. She is married to an Irishman. His mother's people were from Ireland and he has lots of cousins back there, young people and older people I think.
Q: So you think she would put "Irish" down?
A: Yes, probably.
Q: If you were filling it out for them, what would you put?
A: I would put German, French, and Irish.

Ben Richter figured that the children would only answer Irish too, and that they would not mention the other ancestries that he has. Yet he would mention them if he were filling out the census form for them:

Q: What do you think your children would answer on the census form?
A: They would probably say that they were Irish.
Q: Do you think that they would leave out the French and German?
A: I doubt if they even know about the French part, and then if someone asked them, "Why is your name Richter?" I think they would probably remember, "Oh, yeah, I think there is German there."
Q: You think that the Irish part is stronger?
A: I think they hear more about it. Probably from their mother.
Q: If you were filling out the form for them, what would you put down for each kid?
A: Do I have to break it down by eighths and fourths? I can do it. They would be three-eighths German, one-eighth French, and four-eighths Irish. Because they have supposedly 100 percent [Irish] from their mother, so there is half there, plus an eighth from me.[14]

---

14. If Ben is one-eighth Irish and Barbara is 100 percent Irish, the children would logically be five-eights Irish, not the four-eighths Ben gives here.

Q: Do you think you would put all of those things down?
A: I probably would if they asked the question.

I was able to ask only one of the children what he would in fact answer, and 16-year-old Bobby Richter knew all of his ancestries— German, French, and Irish. He was surprised that his parents thought he might answer anything different.

The Albert family is another good example of the complex ways in which information is passed on, lost, and sometimes distorted across generations. Robert Albert, a 60-year-old shipping clerk, is third-generation Italian. His wife, Ellen Albert, a 58-year-old housewife, is second-generation French on her mother's side and fourth-generation Irish on her father's side. Robert Albert was convinced that his two children, aged 33 and 28, would not answer Irish, Italian, and French on the census form. In his words: "I think they are so far removed generationally from everything that they would just probably answer American. I don't think they would mention a particular ethnic group."

Ellen Albert, on the other hand, thought that they might answer Irish, and possibly Italian: "I think they would say Irish and Italian. I think so. But they would not just say Irish and they would not just say Italian. But I think they would just say Irish first. My daughter might just say Italian. I do not know. The French would not even come into the picture."

Their 28-year-old daughter, Janet Albert Parro, a housewife, told me she would answer Italian and Irish. While she was aware of her mother's French background, she did not identify with it at all. She did say that she felt closest to the Irish:

> I feel closer to the Irish. Probably because the people who are in my mom's side of the family have a good sense of humor. You hear the Irish have a nice sense of humor. All of my mom's cousins and relatives are all humorous. They are fun to be with. The Italians are just a different kind. They are just more moody, I think. They are more sentimental types. The Irish—they do not take things as seriously.

In fact, Janet knows the least about the Irish ancestors in her family. She does not know how far back the ancestors were who immigrated here or who they were. She also underestimates the Italian influence on her father as he was growing up. For instance, I asked Janet if either of her parents or grandparents ever spoke a language other than English: "I do not know if my grandmother ever spoke

Italian. She did not around me. Maybe she did when she was younger. My father never knew how to speak Italian, so she probably did not speak it around him." Yet her father, Robert, reports that he did, in fact, speak Italian when he was quite young:

> My grandmother spoke it well. When my mother went to work I was about three or four years old, so my grandmother looked after me, and she taught me how to speak Italian. Both my mom and dad spoke Italian. But when you do not use the language, then you forget it and you get away from it and you can only remember certain phrases and words and things like that. My grandmother taught me, but my parents did not keep it up, so I forgot it entirely. All I remember now are the dirty words.

To sum up, the patterns in the census and survey data as well as the material from the interviews show that ethnic identity can change in both its importance and its content over the life course and intergenerationally. The choices that are made—both conscious and unconscious—are influenced by a variety of factors. These are analyzed in the next chapter.

CHAPTER 3

Influences on Ancestry Choice

The range of choice available to white Americans of European origin about whether or not to identify their ethnic background is quite wide. In a sense they are constantly given an actual choice—they can either identify themselves with their ethnic ancestry or they can "melt" into the wider society and call themselves American. Unlike in the Soviet Union, where people are required to choose an official ethnic identification at the age of sixteen that they keep for life, Americans can, if they choose, change their minds as the situation warrants (Glazer and Moynihan 1975, 17).

THE CHOICE TO BE ETHNIC

One of the most basic choices we have is whether to apply an ethnic label to ourselves. On the census form, the choice is either "Don't Know," "American," or some particular ethnic ancestry. In the 1980 census, 17 percent of the population did not name a specific ancestry. Of these, 6 percent answered "American" or "U.S.," 1 percent gave a religious or unclassifiable response, and 10 percent gave no response (Bureau of the Census 1980a, 1).

The tension between being American and being of a particular ancestry or ethnicity is a complex one. The census form was designed specifically to discourage people from simply answering "American"

52

in response to the ancestry question. If a person answered "American" and also gave some other ancestral group, American was not coded. In the CPS and GSS interviews, the instructions stipulated that if "American" was the response, the interviewer was to continue probing to see if the respondent would ultimately name some ancestral nationality.

Despite this, a sizeable percentage (6 percent) of respondents to the census did give "American" as their ancestry. A still larger number responded "U.S." or "American" in the census reinterview study. While a sizeable number of these people did not know enough about distant family history to provide another ancestry, some proportion are bound to be people who just choose "American" as the ethnicity they most closely identify with.[1]

But most people do identify their ancestry in censuses and surveys. It has long been noted that while people identify as American in a political sense, it has not been adopted as an ethnic identity. With the passage of time and generations from the original immigrants, individuals become progressively assimilated, both culturally and socially. However this does not necessarily mean that they lose their old identity and become "American." As Glazer and Moynihan point out, "Americans become more American and less ethnic all the time. But in the course of participating in this process, they may also simultaneously become more ethnic" (1975, 16).

Margaret Mead discusses this situation in an analysis of the tensions in identification brought about in the United States by the competing principles of the ethic of cultural pluralism versus the ethic of ethnic assimilation. Young people in the United States are encouraged to know about their immigrant roots and to identify with their ancestors, while at the same time the idea of the American national character and the ideal of patriotism are stressed. Mead argues that the sense of being American is never invoked positively for the individual, but rather always in distinction from some other foreign group. Being American, Mead notes, often means staying away from "foreign ways, foreign food, foreign ideas, foreign accents, foreign vices" (Mead 1975, 184, 189).

One can picture the relationship between being American and being of another European ancestry as involving concentric rings of more or less inclusive identity. Individuals conceive of themselves as

1. See Lieberson 1985 for a discussion of the characteristics of this group.

American, and within that as also Irish or German or Polish. In fact, the common names people use when describing their ethnicity reflect this conception of it. People say they are German-American or Irish-American. In most cases the two identities are complementary—you are American but also of German descent. Among the people I interviewed, though, there was a great deal of variation in the weight that people assigned to the component parts of their identification. At one end of the extreme, Anne Gold answered my inquiry about how she would answer the census this way: "Ancestry,...well, I guess I would have said English and Irish...but, well, other than that, American, because we are long-term Americans."

She also reported that she would label her son American, because "otherwise it would just go on forever." Louise Taylor also viewed American as a convenient "backup" ancestry for when things got too complicated with all of her mixed ancestries:

> Q: Do you ever feel any social pressure to have a strong ethnic background?
>
> A: No, because it is so weak in me. It is so far back anyway. You mean roots like everyone else? Well, no, not really. Because if not, you can always fall back on, well, I am American.

At the other extreme was Sean O'Brien, a 52-year-old retired golf pro, who told me in no uncertain terms how important the way he labeled himself was to him:

> I always say I am Irish...I was born and raised in New York City. When we were growing up, we never said we were of Irish ancestry, we just said, "What's your nationality?" I'm Irish. That's it. And when I die, I told Christine, on my tombstone I want her to put, "This Irish S.O.B. had a good time while he was here." That is going on my tombstone. I am not saying this American-Irish, or this American, but this Irishman.

For Maria Reggio, a 46-year-old housewife, and Anthony Donio, a 55-year-old manager, the way one combined "American" and "Italian" said a lot about the degree of importance one attached to one's ancestry. Both of them were very aware of the connotations associated with the placement of the words. Anthony Donio: "You should not say "Italian American." You should say "American of Italian descent." Because an Italian is proud to be an American. Proud of his country. That is a very important part of their character."

For Maria Reggio the placement of the words signifies changes over generations:

Q: Do you think of yourself as American sometimes and as Sicilian or Italian at other times?

A: Yes, I think so. Mostly American. I feel that maybe my generation is Italian, but my children's generation will be Americans more so than myself. Because I was raised in Monterey, we were a community of Italians, so I got that feeling of being an Italian-American. But now we are more American Italian. But probably with my children it will just be American with a background of Italian.

When I asked people about their dual identities—American and Irish or Italian or whatever—they usually responded in a way that showed how they conceived of the relationship between the two identities. Being an American was their primary identity—but so primary that they rarely, if ever, thought about it—most commonly only when they left the country. Being Irish-American, on the other hand, was a way they had of differentiating themselves from others whom they interacted with from day to day—in many cases from spouses or in-laws. Certain of their traits—being emotional, having a sense of humor, talking with their hands—were understood as stemming from their ethnicity. Yet when asked about their identity as Americans, that identity was both removed from their day-to-day consciousness and understood in terms of loyalty and patriotism. Although they may not think they behave or think in a certain way because they are American, being American is something they are both proud of and committed to.

Thus Tim McDaniel, a 68-year-old retired civil servant, is annoyed when people express their Irish ancestry in a way he thinks conflicts with their loyalty to America: "People who have Irish flags in front of their houses. That bothers the hell out of me...If you think you are Irish, then go to Ireland. I love being of Irish descent, but I am an American and I feel that way more than anything."

Since most people understood their American identity in terms of patriotism and nationality, it is not surprising that when I asked them to imagine times when being American and being ethnic could be in opposition, most people mentioned political situations. For many Irish-Americans the trouble in Northern Ireland and their political sympathy for the IRA came to mind. The comments of Bill Hogarty, a 52-year-old salesman, are typical:

Q: Do you think there ever could be a time when being American and being Irish could come into opposition for you?

A: Yes, although I do not approve of the IRA, if all of a sudden the anti-terrorist policy in the U.S. started to use countermeasures against the IRA, I guess I would approve of the policy, but I would definitely be a little worried about it. Although I do not like the IRA, I guess somehow I do identify a little bit with the IRA.

For others like Cindy Betz, a 26-year-old student of Czech and Italian ancestry, the memory of what happened to the Jews in World War II provides an idea of how one can never just blend in as an American and forget one's origins:

> Well, if there is ever a thing like Hitler...he tried to do away with the Jews. I think if that ever happened...like [the] Ku Klux Klan does not like Italians, does not like Catholics...I don't think that would be good if I ran into them. I always think to myself, if the Ku Klux Klan found out that I was Italian, they would kill me. You know, if I ran into them. If something like that happens, I guess no matter what nationality you are, if someone wants to do away with your race, then it is all over.

Most people stressed that their identity as Americans was primary and that they could not imagine a time when it could be in opposition to another identification, but a few recalled the ways in which national sentiment had turned against other ethnic groups in the past. This caused them to wonder about what might happen to them. Susan Badovitch, a 29-year-old librarian, said: "I think that if we ever had some kind of threat of war with Yugoslavia or something, just knowing how weird this country can get, I could see another thing where everybody who had a Slavic name could be in trouble. Like what happened to the Japanese and the Iranians."

Just as some respondents described "falling back on being American" as a way of compensating for not having a strong ethnicity, in a few cases, individuals thought of their ethnic nationality as providing a backup political nationality in case they should ever want an "escape hatch" from being an American. Catherine Masden, a 27-year-old paralegal, told me that her grandmother tried to keep Swiss citizenship in case she needed it for some reason:

> My grandmother had always wanted to hold on to her citizenship from Switzerland. You don't know what is going to happen in the future. It is nice to know that you could go somewhere else. You can flee somewhere else. She would never do that except for safety reasons. Only for the threat of war and stuff. I guess it is something that you do think about.

The Irish government has institutionalized this idea by allowing the third-generation descendants of Irish emigrants to claim Irish citizenship if they should decide they want it. Bill Kerrigan had obviously given this some thought:

When I was age six or something my dad went to the Irish consulate and got some papers. And now anytime I want to declare Irish citizenship I can. I would have to give up my American citizenship, but the knowledge of that makes me feel I can be Irish, even though I won't be Irish, I can be Irish anytime I want. I can move to Ireland, if at any time it looks like a nuclear war, or a war with Nicaragua, and I am opposed to a war with Nicaragua.

Thus the understanding of "American" as a political or national category rather than as an ethnic or cultural category influences the ways in which people see the two identities overlapping or in opposition.

FACTORS INFLUENCING ANCESTRY CHOICE

For most people who are going to choose among different European ancestors in their backgrounds, four factors influence these choices: knowledge about ancestors, surname, looks, and the relative rankings of the groups. Each of these will be examined in turn.

KNOWLEDGE ABOUT ANCESTORS

To decide on one's ethnic identification, one must know what the options are—that is, what ancestries figure in one's genealogy. The level and amount of knowledge and interest an individual has in his or her ethnic ancestry is affected by a number of factors. Some of the more important ones include (1) the socioeconomic status of the family, especially education, (2) the structure of the family (divorce, death, geographic mobility, living arrangements and the effect these have on the level and intensity of contact among family members), and (3) the number of generations the family has been in the United States. All of these factors affect the amount of choice or constraint felt in determining one's ethnic identification and shape the amount of raw material available to the individual to form such an identification.

Several factors affect the intergenerational transfer of information on ethnic ancestry. For the first and second generations, this transfer of information about ethnic origins is not an intentional process but merely a result of socialization. For the third generation and beyond, the process becomes more conscious. Since 56 percent of the population is fourth-generation or more (Smith 1980), and yet 86 percent were able to give a specific ancestry response to a NORC survey and

83 percent to the census (Bureau of the Census 1980a, 1), there must be some degree of intergenerational transfer of information about ancestry occurring. Such information would tend to become more complicated across generations with an increase in intermarriage. Since marriages that unite two native-born whites with the same undivided ethnic heritage form only one quarter of the total marriages among this population (Alba 1985a, 10), the complexity of the information will become greater in the future.

Many more people know about the nativity of their immigrant ancestors than know about other basic characteristics. In a study designed to prove both the reliability and the extent of knowledge respondents have about their ancestors, James Davis and Tom Smith (1980b, 153) report that the nativity of ancestors is the piece of information most likely to be retained across generations. People know more about their parents' birthplaces than they do about their parents' religions, occupations, education, or year of birth. Obviously, nativity of ancestors is a piece of information that families make a point of conveying across generations. Yet the success in conveying such information varies among different families.

Effects of Socioeconomic Status and Education.   Many authors (e.g., Gans 1979) have argued that the maintenance of active ethnic identity and involvement in an ethnic group is related to working-class status, but simple knowledge about one's ancestors is, in fact, related to higher socioeconomic status. Stanley Lieberson (1985) found that it was poorly educated southern rural whites who were most likely to be "unhyphenated whites"—people unable or unwilling to name any specific ancestry. Tom Smith also found that lack of an ethnicity was particularly related to low education. He relates this to the fact that "better educated and better situated family lines are more successful in passing ethnic and other information along to their descendants than lower educated and lower positioned families" (1980, 90). Davis and Smith (1980b) also found that having information about grandparents was positively related to socioeconomic standing in general.[2]

One of the reasons those of higher socioeconomic standing are more likely to retain information about their ancestors' origins is that

2. They also found that Protestants were more knowledgeable than Catholics and Jews about the years of birth, educations, and occupations of their ancestors, whereas non-Protestants were more knowledgeable about their ancestors' religion and ethnicity. This may be the influence of generation.

experience may contribute to an interest in ethnicity and family history (Lieberson and Waters 1986, 14). Many of my respondents, all of whom had at least a high school education, and many of whom had college or graduate degrees, did mention schooling and school projects when they were talking about learning about their family history. For instance, Dan Burke, a 26-year-old lawyer, recalled: "I know a lot about this because when I was in the sixth grade we did the family tree project and so we looked into it then. My family had not done a lot. I mean they knew what their ancestors were basically, but they never sat down and really figured it out, so we did it then. We still have that."

The first point at which there is institutional pressure for ethnic ancestry occurs for many people in grammar school. The expectation in American society that everyone has an ethnic identity in addition to being American is often institutionalized in elementary school projects where children are given the assignment of researching their roots. Many respondents recalled doing a family tree as a homework assignment in grammar school. Susan Badovich remembers that these school assignments reinforced her idea that some ancestries were more common and more socially acceptable than others: "I remember when we got to do ethnic things in class, and they would always say, "Raise your hand, How many kids are Irish? How many Italian?" and the teacher never asked about Slovenian. I was always lumped in the category "Other," and they never asked."

Some respondents, especially those who had attended parochial schools, reported that teasing one another about ethnicity was common when they were in elementary school. School genealogy projects seem to have been universal, at least for respondents under thirty. In addition, it appears to be almost a universal expectation that the family will keep a genealogy, family Bible, or some other record of the family tree. Many respondents pulled out the family Bible in order to respond to questions about ancestors further back than their grandparents.

It was also a common experience for the respondents to have been contacted themselves by some other long-lost relative conducting research into their family tree. Sometimes that experience kindled interest where there had been none before, as in the family of Joyce Hoffman:

When I was in high school my father got a letter from someone in Chicago who had the exact same name who was looking for his roots and wanted to know if my parents knew anything about their background, where the original family came from. I think my parents really tried to dig back at that time. They might have even made some phone calls to other members of the family to figure out more of the details of what they did not know themselves.

Many respondents also said that they had specific information about their grandparents or other ancestors because they had had to get official papers for wills, birth certificates, inheritances, and so on. Families with property to be passed from one generation to another have more reason to keep records than those from a lower socioeconomic background. There may thus be more incentive for wealthier families to transmit information about ancestors and the extended family.

Structure of the Family.   The second factor that affects the passage of information across generations is the structure of the individual's family. Families that remain intact over the life cycle of the individual have more time and opportunity to convey complex information about their ancestry. Families disrupted by divorce, death, or geographic mobility may lose access to both official documents and key informants. So, too, the continued involvement or close link of a family with an aunt or grandparent who is actively interested or involved in his or her ethnic group would have a strong effect on the socialization of the children.

Many of my respondents lacked information about entire sides of their families because they had lost contact with other family members owing to a quarrel or a divorce. A few of the people I interviewed had not been raised by their parents, but rather by aunts, uncles, cousins, or unrelated adults. Thus they had very little information about the side of the family that did not take them in. These people in general knew less about their ethnic backgrounds. This has also been found true in wide-scale social surveys (Smith 1980, 90).

The effect of family structure was very evident in these interviews. A testament to how strong curiosity perhaps is about ethnic origin and family background is the story of Mike Gold, whose parents were divorced when he was quite young. After a series of my questions about his father's side of the family, he finally interrupted and told me that the only time he had ever talked to his father had been on a business trip to the Midwest, when he had looked him up and they had talked for an hour. However, the one thing his father had told him during that brief visit concerned the origins of his last name, and how and by whom it had been changed. It is not surprising that Mike Gold should have few feelings about his father's ethnic background, but he nonetheless now passes on to his children the story about the origins of their family name.[3]

Another example of a similar type is Judy Gray Gilligan, a 44-year-old stockbroker. She was very strongly identified as Serbian, and this maternal ethnicity had been an important influence in her life, overshadowing her father's ancestry:

Q: Are all of your ancestors Serbian?

A: No, just on my mother's side. My parents weren't married. They met during the war in the Fiji Islands. I was born there. I found my father on my own about five years ago after an extensive search through the Pentagon and everywhere else. And I believe that he is of Welsh and British heritage. But I think the maternal identification was so heavy and so much a part of my being that that information about my father did not have much effect. I spent a great deal of time with my grandmother [her mother's mother], who practically raised me. It [the ethnicity] wasn't something I wanted from him. I think I felt that identity so strongly that it didn't occur to me that I had something else.

In a few cases where both parents were present as the children grew up, there still is much less information available about one side of the family because one of the parents is secretive or reluctant to talk about his or her background. The parents of Joseph Bajko, a 20-year-old college student, are an extreme case. He reported that his father was Lithuanian, that he considered himself Lithuanian, and that he would list himself as Lithuanian on the census form. When I asked about his mother, he replied:

Well, I don't know. She refuses to tell anyone what she is. I would gather from her maiden name that she was probably Welsh, because it was Craig and I think that means Cliff by the Sea. So maybe it was English. My grandmother likes to brag that the secret of the family is that someone was Cherokee Indian. At one time or another. We have a thousandth piece of Cherokee Indian someplace in there. I don't know exactly what other ancestries. It could be French. I do know it might be Welsh or English of some sort...I think [my mother's family] lived right near Cajun country ...they could have been Cajun. Yes, she could have been French.

Q: Well what would you answer on the census form?

3. Mike Gold's grandfather was a French immigrant named d'Or. He changed his name by literally translating the word into its English equivalent, Gold.

A: Just Lithuanian because the other is not positive. So why put that
down?

On the other hand, certain family structures and living arrangements may promote both the passage of information about ethnic
origin and the interest in and socialization of children into a particular ethnicity. Often one parent would be much more concerned with
ancestry or ethnic matters than the other. As a result, many respondents were more identified with one side of the family than the other.

Many of those who did strongly identify with a particular ancestry
in their family tree attributed it to a grandparent or other relative who
lived with the family and communicated knowledge and interest in
ethnicity to the young people in the family. In the case of 47-year-old
Christine O'Brien, a third-generation Irish-Italian nurse, her grandmother's influence had strongly reinforced her Italian identity, which
she maintained despite her Irish surname. While Christine believed
that she had been equally influenced by both ancestries, she nevertheless thought that on some occasions she reacted to situations in an
"Italian" way because "my grandmother lived with us for many years
so I think we always tended to go more toward the Italian because she
was so Italian. We were the generation that was starting to break
away, but everything centered around the grandmother." She now sees
herself as fulfilling the same function in her own family—stressing
their Italian side for her children, while letting her husband stress his
Irish ancestry: "Sean transmits the Irish heritage. He is so proud to be
Irish. He would die if he had to change his ethnic background. I try to
make sure the Italian side is brought in because there is so much of it
that I enjoyed growing up."

Generation.   If one side of the family is of a more recent generation,
it sometimes happens that the individual feels closer to that side, but
this was not a consistent finding across all of my interviews. Pat
Quinn, a 20-year-old college student, whose mother is Irish Catholic
and father is Irish Protestant definitely felt closer to her father's
ethnicity, even though she was raised in the Catholic religion. She says
she gets her sense of being Irish from her paternal grandparents, who
immigrated from Northern Ireland:

> I think my mom felt more like she was from San Francisco than anything
> else, just because her whole family had lived there for so long. Since his
> parents were pretty active in the Orange Lodge, my Dad always felt more

Irish. I don't think I really got my sense of being Irish from them. I got it more from my grandparents, whom I spent a lot of time with. My grandmother was the one I went to Ireland with this summer.

Generation may also play a part in the choices of ethnicity. Catherine Masden feels more Swiss than German and Lithuanian because her mother's family much more recently immigrated from Switzerland: "My dad's parents had been here for a long time. They weren't really traditional in their Lithuanian or German customs. I mean I wouldn't even know what they were. Whereas my mom's when we did go there, they had certain foods that they would serve and stuff like that."

People did not always identify with the relative who was the most recent immigrant, however, and neither were the respondents with the strongest ethnic attachment always the closest to the immigrant generation. A few respondents with very strong ethnic identifications were more than four generations removed from the original immigrants. For every case that I found where individuals did accentuate that part of their identity that was closest in generation to the original immigrants, I found one where people did not identify with their most recently arrived relative.

For instance, although Ellen Albert's mother was an immigrant from France who arrived in the United States when she was fourteen, Ellen did not identify as both French and Irish. Rather, she strongly asserted only her Irish identity, despite the fact that she knew far less about that side of her ancestry and had a large number of relatives still living in France:

> I consider myself Irish because I lived in the Mission district and that was Irish. I didn't have any French. My mother was not involved in that. She didn't bother with the neighborhood. I marched in the Saint Patrick's Day parade. The nuns at school were Irish. In third grade the little nun would really give it to you if you didn't have any green on. We would have little green ribbons just in case on the black uniforms. No, I considered myself Irish. I still do. We have Saint Patrick's Day here in this house. We have the biggest party. I have corned beef and cabbage, we make home-baked bread. Now my daughter is making it. And the whole works. The green, even the dogs wear green. I am Irish.

Ellen's 28-year-old daughter, Janet, who was married with three young children and lived in the same parish, about two blocks from her parents' home, reported that she would answer Irish and Italian on the census form because her mother was Irish and her father was

Italian. She had no idea how far back her ancestors who had come from Ireland were or where in Ireland they came from. Her French maternal grandmother, Ellen's mother, had died a few years before. Janet had known her quite well, and so had her two oldest children, but she reported that the French part of her background meant nothing to her. She did, however, identify with her father's side, the Italian part of the family, even though it was a generation removed from her experience. It had been her father's grandparents who had immigrated from Italy, people Janet had never met.

THE CHOICE OF ANCESTRY

As we have seen, many of those who give a response about ancestry on the census form face a choice of which ancestry to respond with. The interviews show that those from mixed ancestral backgrounds use surname and looks to decide which of their ancestries to identify with. Examination of these factors shows how people decide their own self-identification by taking into account how others identify them.

SURNAME

Regardless of whether they believed they were from a homogeneous ethnic background or knew they were from a very mixed ethnic background, some respondents used their surnames to justify their self-identification and to explain how it was that they knew their ancestries. For instance, Louise Taylor used family surnames to describe the different branches of her family. After answering that she would identify herself as Irish-Italian on the census form, she explained why: "My mom's side of the family is part Irish too. Her mother is definitely the Italian part. Then my grandmother's father's name was Flanagan, and so he was the Irish part."

The further they were removed generationally from the original immigrants and the original ethnic influence, the more surnames were used by individuals as clues about their ancestry. Knowledge of mother's or grandmother's maiden name was passed on from generation to generation and used as a symbol or reminder as to where that part of the family had come from.

As far as he could tell, Dan Burke was fourth- or fifth-generation American. He had answered Irish on the census form, and when asked why, he replied, "Because both of my parents are half Irish and so that makes me half Irish." His knowledge about his ancestry was uncertain in many spots and he used the surnames of the relatives he knew about to fill in the gaps. His father's father's family were Irish, Dan claimed by reference to their surname: "They are Irish. They are Fitzpatricks." The Norwegian part of his mother's ancestry was indicated by her maiden name: "Well, my mother also says she is Norwegian too. Definitely, because of her father. Her name was Nelson and that was Norwegian. I think he was 100 percent Norwegian, so that definitely played a part for her. I don't consider myself Norwegian. I know I am part but I would never say I am Norwegian."

The influence of the Norwegian last name, Dan asserted, made his mother identify herself as Norwegian, and he thought she would include Norwegian on the census form. But notwithstanding that the name was a factor for his mother, Dan did not mention his maternal ancestry in his self-identification. He could identify himself as Irish and never have to explain away a Norwegian last name.

The most extreme case of reliance on a surname to fill in for a less than complete family history was that of Joyce Hoffman's family. Joyce answered that she would say German, English, and Scottish on the census form. She most closely identified, however, with the German part of her ancestry, because her mother had consciously decided that the family would be German when Joyce was quite young. This decision to emphasize the family's German heritage was made even though up until that point Joyce's mother had had no idea that the family was German. Joyce explained:

> When I was about eight years old my mother suddenly discovered that we were German. Up until that time for some reason she always thought my father was Irish. She thought he was Irish when she married him. But then this letter came to the house with an extra *n* on the end and my father told her that that was the German spelling of the name and that it was a German name and his grandparents were German. So my mother got really into this and told us all that we were German. She started serving sauerkraut and putting sour cream on top of everything and at night we would get out the atlas and look up Germany and know that we had come from there. It was really sort of bizarre because she didn't even know we were German until this happened but then she got really into it and I really believed that we were German. It was not until I went away to college and met some people who really were members of an ethnic group that I realized that we were not really German.

Even though Joyce had since decided that her mother had been greatly exaggerating the extent of their German ancestry, she still used the surname to conjure up a feeling of ethnic attachment: "Sometimes I think it would be neat if you went back to a town and instead of 1 in every 250,000 people being named Hoffman, there would be a lot of people named Hoffman."

The Effect of Others' Identification.   Some people identified more strongly with one side of their family—the one that matched the ethnicity of their surname—because of the ways in which others used the surname to label them as members of a particular ethnic group. This was true of all of the respondents who had a difficult or unusual last name. For instance, Laurie Jablonski identified herself as part Polish and German in answering the ancestry question. She reported, however, that even though she believed that she was mostly German and only part Polish, she sometimes left out the German ancestry completely:

> Sometimes I just say Polish. It is kind of related to my name. Usually if they were saying, "What is your ethnic background?" I say Polish and German, but I think I just say Polish sometimes.

> Q: Do you feel closer to being Polish than German?

> A: Yes, I do even though I am three-quarters German and only one-quarter Polish. Just because of the last name and being asked about it all of the time. Having to spell it for people. And how people pronounce it. So I am sort of aware of that part of it.

Laurie also reported that the trouble she had with her name was a topic of conversation when she met other people with Polish last names, thus reinforcing her identification as Polish.

Laurie was still unmarried and thought she might very well keep her own name when and if she did marry. One could not help but wonder, however, what would happen to her sense of ethnic identification if her name were to change. Had her identity already been formed to the point where she would continue to identify as Polish, or would she be freed from the effects of ascription by others through her surname and begin to stress her German background? In the rest of the interview, when she was asked about the character traits and cultural practices of the two groups, it was clear that her descriptions of Polish people and practices were largely symbolic, superficial, and reflective of negative media stereotypes of Polish ethnicity. For example, she had bought a mug with a broken handle that had painted on it "Polish coffee mug," and she cited it as an illustration of one of her Polish characteristics. But her descriptions of German relatives, food, and fairs in her native Wisconsin were detailed and culturally complex. In Laurie's case the constraints imposed by her Polish surname were strong enough to overwhelm her firm German cultural identification.

In the case of Christine Fitzpatrick O'Brien, the reverse occurred. She reported that she was third-generation both Irish and Italian and maintained throughout the interview that both ancestries were very important to her. Her father was Irish and her mother Italian, and consequently she had an Irish surname. She saw her mother's Italian extended family quite often as a child, and they had little contact with her father's Irish family. Thus she had managed to maintain both her Italian and her Irish identification despite the influence of her surname.

> I knew I was Italian when I was growing up. It was very obvious that I was Italian. My mother had nine brothers and sisters. I was surrounded by Italians. My father too had nine brothers and sisters, but we saw very little of them. We followed all of the Italian tradition...but it was never drummed into our heads that you were either Italian or you weren't anything. I knew I was Irish too because we celebrated Saint Patrick's Day and we always recognized my father's heritage and the name Fitzpatrick and we marched in the parade. We celebrated both ways.

Perhaps the fact that her mother's family was the more influential in terms of day-to-day tradition counterbalanced the influence of her father's surname. Or perhaps her father's surname and the patrilineal bias were responsible for her keeping both ancestries, and without the influence of the Irish surname she would have given up the Irish part of her self-identification.

People are quite aware of the ways in which others use surnames to label them, and mention of others using their surnames to identify them was a common theme in the interviews. Often people mentioned their surnames when I asked them if it were a common experience for people to ask or comment about their ethnic backgrounds. Cindy Betz is an example: "As soon as they see my last name, they ask me what nationality I am. That is usually the clincher. If I go into a bank, they say, 'How do you pronounce that? What nationality is that?' So I think that is probably why at work, [when] a lot of people see my name, they say, 'What is that?' "

For those whose self-identification corresponds to their ethnic surname, the response of others to the surname may reinforce their pride in their ethnic identification. For example, Tom Scotto:

Q: Is it a common occurrence for people to ask or comment on your ancestry?

A: Yes, of course. In fact when you meet someone new, lots of times they will comment on my last name. It's Sicilian. They'll say, "Oh, you are Sicilian!" Then sometimes they will make a crack about the Mafia. In my shop people will come in and they will make a comment about the fact that I am Italian. When I worked in the phone company or when I was in the Navy guys would tease me about being Italian. It is OK, it is just meant good-naturedly. It is a way of getting to know you. I would know if they meant something bad by it.

When asked whether it was common for others to ask about or comment on their ethnic ancestry, most respondents replied that it was not very common in their day-to-day lives. Most, however, could remember the last time someone had asked, and almost always the stranger or acquaintance had asked about the respondent's surname. Most respondents were very aware of what their name symbolized to others and were accustomed to either saying, "Yes, you guessed correctly" or correcting the wrong impression.

Mike Gold was more concerned about why people commonly asked him about his last name, not because he suspected that they would guess that he was English, Scottish, and French, but because he was sure that they were trying to discover whether he was Jewish or not: "A lot of times when I am on the phone with somebody and they ask my name, they ask me how to spell it because they want to know if it is spelled Gould instead of just Gold, which I think means they want to know whether I am a Jew or not."

In fact, Gold's concern reflects the fact that while almost everyone is aware of the extent to which surnames are used to determine ethnic ancestry, everyone also knows what unreliable indicators surnames are. There are three factors that undermine the reliability of surnames as a predictor of ancestry: intermarriage, name changes, and changing sensitivity in society to types of surnames. Each of these is considered below.

Intermarriage.   The first problem in using surnames to ethnically identify people is intermarriage. A surname commonly indicates only the paternal side of the ancestral line. Children are usually given their fathers' surnames and wives generally take those of their husbands, so that it is in fact relatively difficult to trace one's origins through the maternal line.

When husband and wife are from the same ethnic group, the husband's name is a valid marker of the ethnicity for the whole family. If your maiden name is Gallucci and your married name is Pontucci, those judging your ethnicity from your surname will come to the same conclusion whichever you use. However, in the case of marriage across ethnicities, the surname becomes an unreliable marker of ethnic ancestry because it only gives information on one side of the family. Yet since it is still widely used in our society to determine ethnicity, it has a strong effect on self-identification. People know that others use their surnames to assign them to particular ancestries and sometimes self-identify correspondingly.

The effect of intermarriage on the accuracy of labeling via surname is evident in the remarks made by Sean O'Brien about his wife. Proud of his Irish heritage, he joked about the fact that he never would have dated or married his wife if her father had been Italian and her mother Irish, giving her an Italian surname, rather than the way that it was: an Irish father, Italian mother, and Irish surname: "I tease Christine...She is half Irish and half Italian and her maiden name is Fitzpatrick. That's the only reason I asked her out because she had an Irish last name. If her last name had been Italian, I probably never would have asked her out."

A similar story was told by Bonnie Ostrowski, a 50-year-old housewife, whose immigrant parents were quite insistent that she date only Polish boys. Her future husband was Polish, German, Scottish, and Irish, but had a Polish last name, which allowed her to date him even though he was not "pure" Polish: "The only person I ever was serious about was my husband and his name was right... even if he was German, Scottish and Irish, he was Polish!" Bonnie thought it quite ironic that people guessed her to be Polish based on her husband's last name, when she was in fact more Polish than he was.

Married women are often mistakenly assigned the ethnicity associated with their surnames, which are actually their husband's surnames. This can have different consequences, depending on the type and level of ethnic identity of the women involved. Some women who were very strongly ethnically identified had some of that identity muted by a less identifiable surname. For instance, Judy Gray Gilligan, who grew up going to Serbian summer camps and observing many Serbian customs, feels very close to her Serbian roots and is proud of her Serbian heritage. Yet when I asked her if she felt Serbian sometimes and American at other times, she replied: "Well, because my last name has been Gray for the last twenty years, I think of myself as an American. I think the only time that the Serbian enters it is when I am at a Serbian function or I am among my family and they expect me to be Serbian, and then my identity shifts a bit."

Elaine Williams, a 32-year-old office worker, is of wholly Italian background, but married a man of English background with the last name of Williams. Since she no longer has an Italian last name, fewer people ask her about her background:

Q: Is it a common occurrence for people to ask or comment on your ethnic background?

A: No, not now that my name is not Italian. Because apparently I do not look real Italian. But before I was married, when people would learn my name, they would say, "Oh, you are Italian." And, if they were too, then we would discuss being Italian together. But I don't find that as much now.

On the other hand, sometimes a name change as the result of being married gives a woman who had no particularly strong ethnic background the chance to be considered "ethnic" by others. Liz Field, a 35-year-old weaver, who is now divorced, but had an Italian last name when she was married, observed:

I had more fun with my name when it was DeCinci. People were always saying, "How do you spell that?" and "Are you Italian?" Some people just assumed I was Italian...an old Italian woman who was a friend's grand-mother tried to prove to me that I was Italian...she was absolutely positive...

Name Changes.   The second problem with using a surname as an indication of ancestry is that it may have been changed. There is a long history of surname changes in the United States. Many immigrants had their names changed for them by immigration or other officials. Other immigrants or their children changed their names on purpose to make them sound less ethnic.

Many of the people I interviewed had names that had been changed at some point by their ancestors. For instance, the Albert family knew that their name had once been Alberti. Bob Albert's grandfather had changed it when he first immigrated to Louisiana from Sicily. Bob Albert thinks it was changed in order to escape discrimination:

> My grandfather's name was Alberti. For one reason or another he dropped the *i* from the name, so our name was Albert. It has been that way ever since, so my dad was born Albert. I kind of presume that maybe it was for business reasons because down in Louisiana there were a lot of French people and maybe he wanted to be in business and maybe he wanted to make them think that he was French rather than Italian.

Janet Albert Parro, his 28-year-old daughter, was convinced that because her name had been changed, she had been spared a great deal of teasing in elementary school. She recounted many stories of children with complicated Italian names who were ridiculed by other children. "I had a girlfriend, her last name was Poppilissio. That made the kids hysterical...But I didn't have an Italian last name." Janet was in effect "passing" as non-Italian while the other children were making fun of those with Italian last names.

Knowledge of Surnames. The third way in which the use of surnames to determine ethnic identity can lead to error involves misidentification with the wrong ethnic group. The association of a particular surname with a particular ethnic group is the result of a learning process. As children grow up, they learn what is considered a typical Irish or Italian or Dutch name. They also learn through individual experience to associate the surnames of people they know with the ancestry they know the other person identifies with. This learning process admits of many potential errors and misidentifications, which may well vary by ethnic group.

Two respondents described this type of confusion. Lisa Paulo, a 24-year-old bank teller, was sure that hers was a well-known Portuguese surname. She reported, however, that others often thought it was Italian. Janet Albert Parro reported the same type of error with her husband's Spanish last name—an ironic twist, since Janet herself had escaped identification as Italian when she was young because her father's family had changed their name from Alberti to Albert. Many other people also said they were often misidentified as Irish or Italian, two of the most common and widely recognized groups. Bonnie Ostrowski reported that a paper boy had once tried to make her name Irish by billing a Mrs. O'Strowski.

Even when people use surnames to figure out their *own* ancestry, they are at risk of making a mistake based on misidentifying other surnames. For example, Rose Peters:

Q: What would you put on the census form?

A: Italian and Irish. That is not really complete. I can give you a list, but that would have been my answer.

Q: What else is there?

A: Welsh, English, and Lithuanian. I just found this out recently. I was raised thinking I was half Italian and half Irish.

Q: How did you find out?

A: Well, in 1981 I guess I took a sociology course and the teacher assigned us to find out about our last names. I based it on my maiden name and I thought it was Irish and I went home and told my father and he got in this big huff and said, "No, it's Welsh." All this time I thought it was all Irish.

The ways in which people came to misidentify names are varied. In many cases it may be that a name actually does originate in another ethnic group, which the individual does not think his or her ancestors are from. Perhaps generations ago on the paternal side, Lisa Paulo's ancestor was an Italian who went to Portugal. Or possibly because the Portuguese are a much less numerous group in the United States, there is a lack of knowledge of the structure of their names among the general public. Since they look and sound similar, people generally lump together Portuguese and Italian names.

The process whereby people learn to associate individual names with ethnic groups is also subject to error. Dan Burke, whom we encountered earlier using his knowledge of family surnames to fill in some missing ancestral history, must have received some information from his family about what constitutes an Irish name. But if that information or line of reasoning is wrong, Dan is trapped in a logical fallacy. He knows his ancestors to have been Irish, and he knows some of their names, so he has come to believe that the names themselves are Irish, a fact he then takes for further proof of how Irish his relatives are: "My grandfather's name was Dion, which was very Irish, and that is also my oldest uncle's name, and so that is why I have an Irish impression: a lot of the names seem Irish. I know Dion is. Ivan, I don't know if that is Irish. I think it is."

Dan thus both uses the claim that his relatives are Irish to interpret their names and the supposition that those names are Irish to label his relatives. It may in fact be true that his relative Ivan is Irish, but there is no necessary connection there.

The Use of Surnames to Label Others. Although people frequently recognize that surnames are not always reliable indicators of their *own* ethnic identities, they are not prevented by this from using surnames to label others. The realization that determination of one's own ancestry is not necessarily straightforward does not inhibit the assumption that the situation is uncomplicated for others.

Many people spoke of a warm feeling that they got when meeting someone who shared their ancestry. This affinity existed even though at other points in the interviews these same respondents observed that their own surnames were not accurate indicators of their ancestry. Sean O'Brien reported his response to anyone with an Irish surname:

> I think I am a firm believer that you take care of your own. Probably I am prejudiced in a way that I might give an Irishman a second look before I would give a break to someone else, with some other ethnic background. I am a little prejudiced when it comes to that. Because he is Irish, he gets a little more. He could be ten generations away, but the name is everything. I might give an Irishman the edge.

O'Brien's preference for the Irish was also mirrored in what he perceived as others giving him special treatment just because of his Irish name. He recounted this story from his days in the Navy:

> I can remember when I was in the Navy and I was in Auckland, New Zealand. There were hundreds and hundreds of sailors around. I was in this pub, playing darts with this guy and he said his name was Eddie O'Leary. He asked me what my name was, and I said Sean Patrick O'Brien. Well, for three weeks I could not buy a drink and nobody could look at me. Eddie O'Leary was about six foot six and 300 pounds and Eddie took me under his wing and nobody could look cross-eyed at me because I was Sean Patrick O'Brien and he was Eddie O'Leary transplanted from Ireland someplace.

Sean O'Brien's affection for Irish names also made him a Boston Celtics fan because of the name of the team.

Susan Badovich reported the same feeling of affinity when she met other people who might be Slovenian. Again, she judged their ethnicity based on their surnames: "It is always exciting if someone has an *ich* at the end of their name. I always think, oh, well, maybe they are from Yugoslavia. And so there is a real kindred feeling with meeting other people that have the same kind of name and it is exciting for me to tell them that my grandparents are from Yugoslavia."

The ways in which others use surnames to identify individuals as

being of a particular ethnicity was made clear to me in the responses
people gave to a series of questions I asked on the ethnicity of various
members of their social networks. I asked everyone what the religion
and ethnic origins of their dentist, doctor, lawyer, and priest were.
Most people did not know most of the answers right away. But many
attempted to guess by musing about the possible meanings of their
names. For instance, Barbara Richter replied: "My doctor, his name is
Van Dyke, I imagine he must be German or Dutch or something like
that."

John Davis, a 32-year-old machinist, remembers his thinking as a
child when he discovered that his parents could figure out people's
ancestries by using surnames: "Because I remember when I was young
sitting around with my parents. Just by the different names they heard
they could tell whether they were Irish or English or whatever and I
remember being a little bit amazed that you could learn that."

People also used surnames to determine the ethnicity of close
friends and relatives. For instance, Rich Cahill, a 29-year-old policeman, was explicit about using surnames to determine the ethnicity of
his friends, so he could answer my question:

> Let's see, Sasha, his mother is East German. His last name is Racoeur, so
> his father is probably French or something. William Davis, I do not know
> what his parents are. I don't know what kind of name Silver is, but he is
> adopted. He says he is Italian. I don't know if he has been raised Italian.
> Paul is Japanese; he is a very good friend. I am trying to figure this out by
> last names. Then that also helps me to remember what they said their
> origins were. Constantino, he is Italian and I think English. Interesting, I
> am not sure if he is English.

When I asked Laurie Jablonski whether any of her aunts and uncles
had married out of the ethnic group, she also needed me to help her
even decide what the ethnicities of some of their spouses were: "I
don't think anybody is married to anyone else who is Polish. And one
aunt's name is Scott. Is that English or something? My other aunt
married a Nicholson. I don't know what that is, Norwegian or
something."

While the confusion and guesswork about the ancestry of even
close friends and relatives does say quite a bit about the relatively
little meaning attached to ethnicity, it also shows the continuing ways
in which people are identified by others through surnames. It is not as
if the majority of my respondents thought names *should* be a reliable

marker of ethnicity, but rather just that they *used* them as such. Some respondents, for example, recognized that many black people have last names that can be considered Irish. I asked Betty O'Keefe whether being Irish ever influenced her voting behavior, and she responded: "When I am really at a loss, and I really don't know anything about [the candidates] I just vote Irish. But usually when I vote for someone named O'Brien, it turns out to be a black O'Brien."

Surnames are not, however, the only marker used to identify ethnicity. It is also common to judge by physical appearance.

THE USE OF PHYSICAL APPEARANCE

The belief that one is a member of an ethnic group because of descent from common ancestors implies that one shares a certain amount of genetic material with one's fellow ethnics. This leads to the logical presumption, often true in practice, that members of the same ethnic group will resemble a certain physical type. When groups that form ethnic units are endogamous, it is true that they generally tend to look alike, although using physical appearance to identify any particular person—even one of "pure" ancestry—is never completely automatic. When groups have been in contact for a long time and intermarriage has occurred, physical appearance is a less reliable way of identifying in- and out-group members. Individuals are nonetheless aware of their own physical appearances and of how closely they resemble stereo-types of their ethnic group.

The determination of what physical characteristics serve as markers of ethnicity is a complex process, and the attributes chosen can vary from place to place. As Pierre van den Berghe points out, people tend to walk around with an image or "mental picture of what a model group member looks like" (1985, 58). Such models are accepted by both insiders and outsiders and are often used to judge instanta-neously whether a person is a member of your own ethnic group. The degree to which physical appearance is used to determine one's ancestry affects the ease with which a person moves into or out of the group. A person who closely matches the stereotype of his or her ethnic group is easily typecast. It also can constrain an individual's choice of which of various ancestries to identify with. If one believes one is "marked" as Italian as opposed to Irish, one will tend to identify with Italians.

Italians typify changing perceptions of ethnicity in the United States. Richard Alba notes that southern Italians were seen as a different race by Americans when they first immigrated:

> Astonishing as this may seem in the light of contemporary racial perceptions, many Americans doubted that Italians were whites. Illustrative is the reply of one man when asked during his appearance before a Congressional Committee if he considered the Italian a white man. "No sir, an Italian is a Dago." (Alba 1985b, 68)

Italians, according to Alba, were described as "swarthy" people with low foreheads who stood out by virtue of their dark complexions. However, as Italians became more accepted politically and socially into the American mainstream, their physical differences were not perceived as so radically different.

Those I interviewed were aware of how others used their physical appearances to estimate their ethnicity or ancestry. To a very great extent, they carried around mental images of what various ethnic groups look like. And they often used these images and their understanding of their own physical appearances to choose which branch of their family or which of their possible identities they could use to self-identify.

Robert Albert said it was common for people to identify him as Italian, despite the fact that his surname was changed and no longer serves as a marker:

> In the line of work that I am in, which is merchandising in supermarkets, I deal with a lot of Italians and they know I am Italian.
>
> Q: How do they know?
>
> A: Well, I think just looking at me, they can just tell.
>
> Q: Can you tell another Italian person?
>
> A: Yes, pretty much so... either by their coloring or if they have a big nose like mine, just by their face and features. Now you look like you might be of Irish heritage.[4]

Similarly, both Patricia Quinn and Dan Burke are identified by others as Irish, but they are unclear as to how much of it is the surname and how much of it is looks. Since they both think they look Irish and have Irish names, the two markers function to reinforce their Irish identity, even though Burke, for example, is less than half Irish.

---

4. Mr. Albert was congratulated for correctly guessing the author's ethnic ancestry.

As Pat Quinn states, often when she meets new people it will come up that she is Irish: "I guess people always thought I looked Irish, and my last name is Quinn. People would always say, 'Oh, you must be Irish, look at all of those freckles.'"

These respondents were unusual though, because with the large number of name changes and high rates of intermarriage among this population, more often than not the markers of names and physical appearance do not agree. For Christine O'Brien, her Italian appearance is so noticeable that it causes people to remark about the disparity between her appearance and her surname: "Well, my married name is O'Brien and occasionally people will say, 'What is this? You are not Irish, look at you.' It is obvious that I have some Mediterranean blood in me."

The fact that the relative balance of these forces of choice and constraint vary from person to person is evident when Christine O'Brien's experience is contrasted with Louise Taylor's. The latter also reported herself as Irish and Italian on the census form, but unlike Christine O'Brien, she does not think that others identify her using either her surname or her appearance. Thus she is freer to pick and choose her self-identification from among the ethnicities in her background without fear of being challenged.

Many respondents recognized how unreliable a marker physical appearance is. They were able to cite many instances in which other people had misjudged their ethnicity. For instance, Catherine Masden, who is of Swiss, German, and Lithuanian descent, reported the following incident: "Someone just said to me the other day, 'What are you besides Italian?' I looked at them and said, 'I am not Italian.' They said, 'You are too!'"

Maria Reggio, a Sicilian-American, reported that she was often assumed to be Greek because of her appearance. Lisa Paulo pointed out that often she herself could not even recognize another Portuguese:

Q: Can you spot another Portuguese person when you see one?

A: Not always. Because a lot of the time the features are really similar to either a light Italian or a light Spanish person or a Mexican. When we first moved to Union City, all of the Mexicans loved my sister because they thought she was Mexican. I could probably say she looks Portuguese, but I can't necessarily tell.

The better known in a particular area an ethnic group is, the more likely that people will recognize its "typical" physical appearance. But the less common ethnic groups are less easily recognized. John Davis says that people do not readily identify him as Czech, because "if you look at someone you can't tell if they are Czech or not. Most people don't know."

Despite the fact that so many respondents had so much experience with misidentification and reported so much intermarriage and ethnic mixing in their past, the overwhelming majority of my respondents did feel that they could spot another person of their ancestry group, although the degree of confidence people felt in their predictions varied quite a bit. Those who recognized how easily intermarriage and other factors led to misidentification qualified their answers to this question or said they would be careful when guessing the backgrounds of people they met.

The fact that people are aware they could be wrong does not stop them from doing it. For instance, Carol Davis, a 32-year-old technical artist, guesses about other people sometimes even though she knows she may not be correct:

Q: Can you spot another Irish person?

A: I think so, yeah, to a certain point.

Q: How can you tell?

A: I think coloring has a lot to do with it, and even though some Irish have a lot of dark hair, just coloring. And it wouldn't be all the time, because there are some people who are Jewish that I would swear they are Irish. Other than that you can't really tell.

She notes that people often guess that she is Irish—she thinks because of her looks but sometimes ironically because of her married last name—which is not Irish at all but English in origin. She thinks that sometimes people incorrectly identify the name as Irish, thus correctly identifying her as Irish.

Cindy Betz seemed confused also about her ability to spot an Italian:

Q: Can you spot another Italian?

A: Nowadays you really can't because there are so many different people and so many people who are Jewish or Greek look Italian. If you go into South Philly, nine out of ten people are going to be Italian, and they look Italian, and you know because they live there. But I think that now it is sort of hard to judge. It is weird how people have just interbreed. I think a lot of people might have a little bit of something in them which makes them look like Italian. But I think you could pretty much spot someone if they were all Italian. Or if someone was Jewish or if they looked Greek. I think you could sort of tell. Not a whole lot. But if you could go out on the street and you look I think you could sort of tell but you may be wrong.

Q: Do you ever do that?

A: If I see someone, I will ask them what their nationality is. Then if they say something else, I don't say, "Oh, I thought you were Italian."

Most respondents were not very clear about how they identified ethnicity through appearance. Most mentioned some sort of instinctual feel for knowing another person of their same ancestry, and often of other ancestries too. Ellen Albert, who identified with her Irish ancestry, reported that she could not spot another Irish person when she saw one, but that she was able to tell Italians and Portuguese. She was confident she could make this determination based on a very tenuous connection: "Most of the time, I can tell Portuguese too. Portuguese have the most beautiful skin, even the men. My cousin on my father's side is half Portuguese. So I knew Portuguese people."

Suzanne Benson, a 47-year-old clerk, told me that it was easy to spot Italian men, but harder to spot the women. The characteristics she used to make this determination were as follows: "For Italians the guys wear a lot of gold and they have dark hair and they have a lot of hair all over them."

Joan Cahill, a 24-year-old account representative, seemed to believe she could identify Irish people through a process of elimination. If she saw someone not identifiable as a member of another ethnic group, she assumed they were Irish:

If I see a redhead or something I'll be thinking, "Oh, he looks so Irish and all." I guess I can because I know if they are not Irish—you know like if they look Italian or something. I do have a picture of what the Italians look like. They have darker skin, dark hair, they talk a lot with their hands, they talk with accents.

The attributes most commonly mentioned when I insisted on asking how it was that they could spot another ethnic were skin, hair, and eye color. It seemed almost miraculous to me that most of these people claimed to be right most of the time when they made these guesses, especially since they sometimes gave quite different descriptions of the same ethnic group. One claimed he could tell another Irish person based on pale skin and dark hair, while another said he based his guess on ruddy complexion and red hair. The fact that both claimed to be right all of the time either means that they were running into very different types of Irish people, or perhaps that they had trouble articulating the "instinctual" way they found fellow Irish people.

Tim McDaniel articulated the contradictions that arise when you try to get people to say how exactly they can tell whether a person is of a particular ancestry:

> Sure, I can tell other Irish. I can tell by their features usually. Mainly, well in the Philadelphia area anyway, they are mainly big people. I imagine that was a selective something when they came over, they wanted a gardener or a chauffeur or a houseman. They wanted a great big guy that was imposing so that's what they picked. Now I'm surprised when I go to high school reunions and things that there are mainly Irish people that go and there are so many short people, because I figure I am short...I was five foot ten and, well, I was short. But some of those people are only five feet six or so. So I guess it all depends where you are from, but normally Irish people are big, or else they are really small. There doesn't seem to be any in between. And their heads aren't the same as Germans and Polish. I can usually tell them apart because they have different shaped heads. Matter of fact I can tell Sicilians from other Italians too.

Most people, however, refused to be pinned down on how they made these determinations. They fell back on saying something like, "I don't know; sometimes you can just tell," or, "I don't know what it is. It is something." For Mary McGowan, a 60-year-old day-care worker: "I do not know. It is just instinct or something. And I have been around them so long. The way they look or the way they act or something. It is like with nuns and priests. You can spot them even when they are out of uniform."

It is likely that individuals are making these guesses based not actually on physical appearance alone, but on various mannerisms, gestures, or body language, which varies among ethnic groups, and which people are unaware of. Such learned behavior as intonation of speech, posture, and so forth may be so subtle that people do not notice it consciously, but may nonetheless provide clues as to ethnic origin. Since people are unaware that they use such markers, they may attribute their ability to guess someone's ethnic background to physical appearance.

Often when someone else is spotted as coming from the same ethnic group, it engenders a feeling of affinity in much the same way a recognizable surname does. This happens even though those who report feeling such an affinity are also quite aware that names and looks are unreliable indicators of ancestry. As noted earlier, Susan Badovich reported that she was excited when she met another person of Yugoslav origin. She claimed she could spot them by their appearance: "Part of it is the name, and now that I am more aware of it, I can almost tell by the way people look." Patrick O'Connor automatically felt a sense of kinship with someone who he thought might be Irish: "If I see someone who is Irish, I'll usually make a note and say to myself, 'Oh, good, there is an Irish person.' If I can spot that the person is really ethnic then I think, 'This person knows what I am and he recognizes what I have done and haven't done. I feel like we can understand each other.' "

The belief that looks and inherited traits were shared by everyone labeled with the same ethnicity persisted among the people I interviewed—even though, as I have shown, many of them knew of recent ancestors of a different ancestry than the one the respondent self-identified with.

Respondents were also aware of how others thought they looked, and this too affected their ethnic identification. For instance, Janet Albert Parro had an apparently WASP maiden name and her mother was French and Irish. She could theoretically have simplified to her mother's ancestry, especially since she preferred her Irish side to any of the others. However, since she believed that she "looked" Italian and that others would identify her as Italian even if she did not self-identify that way, she identified strongly with the ancestry of both of her parents.

RANKINGS OF ETHNIC GROUPS

The other major factor that influences which elements of one's ancestry one chooses to identify with is one's perception of the relative rankings of the ethnic groups themselves—the issue of which ethnic groups are more socially acceptable than others. My interviews indicate that people do perceive certain of their available ancestries as more or less attractive than others.

Some people choose to identify with an ancestry based on stereotypes or concepts they have about the desirability or undesirability of one ancestry or another. Ben Richter, whom we encountered earlier, had only a very tenuous ethnic identity. He could not explain why he identified more with his German side, but had definite ideas about the different groups:

Q: Would you say that being Irish and French and German is important to you?

A: I am not sure. I guess I never thought the French part was such a good idea. The Irish part, I don't know. I probably was more fond of the German part.

Q: Why?

A: Well, I don't know. I think they tend to be a little sharper in some ways, and they seem to be more determined than some of the other nationalities.

Q: More determined than the Irish and the French?

A: I think so.

Q: What do you mean by determined?

A: Determined to get something, to win the prize or to get the goal.

Q: Why are you not as fond of the French part?

A: I don't know. Frenchmen just don't turn me on.

Ben was responding to the positive connotations he associated with German ancestry. Louise Taylor sifted through her ancestries based on the negative stereotypes she held of various ancestries. She reported that she would have answered Irish and Italian on the census. When asked why, she replied:

Well, on my mother's side, her great-grandmother was born in Italy. But we have been in California for a long time. I think I am something like sixth-generation Californian or something. And then I guess her father is Irish. And then my father is Irish.

Q: Do you know who among his relatives came here and when?

A: Somebody on his mom's side, and his dad is actually English too and a little Scottish.

Q: Why would you not have said Irish, Italian, English and Scottish?

A: Well, I don't know. I guess probably because I know more about the Irish part.

Later in the interview it became clear that at least the Scottish part of her ancestry was consciously suppressed and downplayed on purpose within the family. She told me that her last name was Scottish, but that the family "tried not to think of it that way." She also reported that whenever anyone in her family was teased about being cheap, that the family would claim that it was their Scottish ancestry showing. Scottish was an ancestry that many people refused to identify with, even though they knew that an ancestor of theirs had been from Scotland.[5] For instance, Sean O'Brien, who is quite proud of his Irish heritage, points out his own bias:

> I always say I am Irish. Because I am proud to be Irish. On my father's side, my grandmother was born in Ireland and my grandfather was born here in the United States. On my mother's side, her mother was born in Ireland and her father was born in Scotland.
>
> Q: Do you ever say you are Scottish?
>
> A: No, I never say I am Scottish.
>
> Q: Why?
>
> A: We used to tease my mother about being part Scottish...we said, "I am not telling anyone I am part Scottish because they are so cheap," and all that. We teased my mother, it got to be a habit, a family joke.

Recall from chapter 2 that Scottish was also an unpopular ancestry for parents labeling children. In changes reported on the relative rankings of ethnic groups in the Bogardus Social Distance Scale over the period 1926 to 1977, Scottish did decline in relative popularity. It had a score of 1.13 in 1926, which put it in fourth position, and fell steadily thereafter, scoring 1.26 (fifth place) in 1946, 1.60 (seventh place) in 1956, 1.53 (ninth place) in 1966, and 1.83 (ninth place) in 1977 (Owen et al. 1981, 84–87).

Other Political Considerations. Many people cited various political or social events as having an effect on their consciousness and degree of ethnic identity. I have already noted Laurie Jablonski's stronger identification with her Polish than with her German ancestry, a fact she attributed to the influence her surname had on how others reacted to her. When I asked about times when the relative influence of one or the other side might be stronger or weaker, however, she revealed that political events in Germany and Poland had a lot to do with how she chose to identify herself:

5. Recall from chapter 2 that Scottish was also by far the most unpopular ancestry label to give children. The reluctance of my sample to mention that they were of Scottish ancestry may be because of the sample selection. I interviewed only Catholics, and there may be a special reluctance on their part to admit to having Scottish ancestry because of its association with Protestantism. However, the fact that the census data show Scottish to be an unpopular ancestry, and the fact that many of my respondents associated it with being "cheap," or some other undesirable stereotype, may mean that there is in fact a bias against Scottish ancestry in the United States.

I guess when the whole thing with Solidarity happened and martial law in Poland and I sort of thought about that and I wondered if I had any relatives over there. I kind of felt some affinity to the people over there and that was the first time I felt conscious of being Polish and what being Polish was. More than just this stupid name I had to spell all the time. So that was kind of a time when I felt more aware of it and it was more real to me.

The warm feelings of affinity that she describes when reacting to the events in Poland are exactly opposite to the feelings of disassociation she felt in reference to Germany:

Q: Did you ever have a similar feeling about being German?

A: [Laughs.] When Hitler took over. [Laughs again.] Not really. One time when I worked as a counselor at a group house, one of the women there was really mad at another counselor and was describing her to other residents as being German. Then I started thinking, "Oh, God, people think of Germans as being like Nazis and being cold people," and it sort of hit me in a way like it had not hit before. I did not want to identify with that at all. I thought, "God, I am not really German." It seemed like an awful thing to say then to be German. Like an insult for people to describe you as German.

The association of being German with being a Nazi is still strong for Laurie, forty years after World War II. A story similar to Laurie's is related in a description by Hinda Winawer-Steiner and Norbert Wetzel of a workshop for family therapists on ethnicity and family therapy. The therapists were supposed to talk about their ethnicity and how it might influence their work. A discussion of a German-American family in therapy revealed that two of the therapists who had identified themselves as Polish-American at the beginning of the workshop, were, in fact, half German. It turned out that they were suppressing their German identity because of the negative connotations associated with being German. "When asked, one explained that she simply considered herself Polish. The other, after some reflection, said that in a group that was half Jewish, she had been reluctant to acknowledge her German heritage" (Winawer-Steiner and Wetzel 1982, 253).

These incidents show how people take into account the group they are interacting with and its possible beliefs. It was not that Laurie associated being German with being Nazi, or that she never admitted to being German in any situation because she was ashamed of it. Rather, she understood that among certain audiences, being German would not be well appreciated. So, too, the psychotherapist realized that in a group of Jewish people, being German might lead others to have a negative opinion of her. In both cases the situation the individual found herself in had a determining influence on her choice of ethnic identification. The effect of the Nazi movement and World War II was still quite strong in the 1980s in terms of popular perceptions of the German-American character. This must have had an enormous effect on German-Americans' ethnic identity during the period close to the war. Winawer-Steiner and Wetzel conclude that it has shaped the entire experience of being German-American:

> World War II left German Americans with almost nothing positive with which they could identify. Germans had committed barbarian, atrocious crimes and Germany was the outcast among the nations of the world. One's Germanness, therefore, out of necessity, had to be toned down and at the very least, experienced carefully and secretly. Ethnic origin for German Americans may be associated with a profound loss of ethnic identity and pride. (1982, 253)

Other respondents mentioned political events and occurrences that had made them more aware or prouder of their ethnic ancestry. Bonnie Ostrowski felt a special surge of pride when they chose a Polish pope, and the Scottos reported a special feeling of accomplishment when Geraldine Ferraro ran for vice president. Rather reluctantly, their son Pete also reported feeling proud of Ferraro.[6] Other Italian-American respondents reported feeling proud of New York Governor Mario Cuomo.

The political significance attached to particular ethnic categories can cause people to change the way they label themselves. An example of a very complex labeling process is the case of Irish Protestants and Irish Catholics. At times "Irish" may be understood as a category that includes both Catholic and Protestant. In the political situation in Northern Ireland, the distinction between Catholics and Protestants is at the heart of the political split. Thus, depending on the situation, Irish Protestants may identify themselves simply as Irish or may stress that they are Scots-Irish, Irish Protestant, or British in an attempt to differentiate themselves from Irish Catholics. In the Current Population Survey, respondents who called themselves Scots-Irish were put into the "English, Scottish, Welsh" category. In the 1980 census

---

6. Such feelings of pride, and the resulting attention they paid to Ferraro's campaign, did not translate into ethnic loyalty votes in either case. Though they were glad to see Ferraro run for office, Rose and Tom Scotto voted for Ronald Reagan in the presidential election, and Pete supported Jesse Jackson in the Democratic primary.

coding, however, those who gave Northern Ireland as their ancestral place of origin were included in the Irish category.

I asked people who gave their ancestry as Irish whether they thought people from Northern Ireland should be considered Irish. There was some disagreement among my respondents. Mary Mc-Gowan said that Irish people were all the same and that if she met a Protestant from Northern Ireland, she would "invite them in and give them a drink." Others echoed her sentiments and claimed that anyone who called themselves Irish should be considered Irish. A few respondents were puzzled at my question and argued that if there was such a big problem over there, there must be some big difference between Irish Catholics and Irish Protestants, although they really did not know what it was.

Some Irish Catholics I interviewed had definite feelings, however, that Irish Protestants were not to be considered Irish. Pat O'Connor: "I've met some that I do consider Irish, but on a sort of instinctual level, no, they are not Irish. Let them go back to England." In the case of Bill Kerrigan and Patricia Quinn, two suburban Californians, this lack of agreement in labeling could lead to some problems. Pat Quinn's father's family is Irish Protestant and her mother's is Irish Catholic. She was raised Catholic, yet feels Irish because of the influence of her paternal grandparents, who were immigrants from Northern Ireland. The split between Catholics and Protestants caused a lot of problems in her own family when her parents married. She no longer feels any big distinction between the Catholics and Protestants, however, and answered all of my questions by referring to her Irish ancestry.

However, her boyfriend, Bill Kerrigan, is from a fiercely Irish Catholic family. His father used to send guns to the IRA and his grandfather was involved in the Easter Uprising in 1916. Bill has never told Pat this, but he does not consider her father's side of the family to be Irish:

> For some reason it is hard for me to think that the Quinns, as opposed to the Fitzgeralds [her mother's side]—that the Quinns are really Irish, for some reason. I do not know why, they just do not seem Irish. Irish has to be Catholic. Somewhere in my mind it has to be Catholic. The Protestants are just imposters. I always think of them as Scottish, the Protestants are Scottish colonists, and whether or not they have lived there for three hundred years, they are still Scottish.

Even as far removed from the Irish conflict as two suburban Californian young adults, it is clear that there are political connotations to self- and other ethnic identification. In the case of Irish Protestants and Irish Catholics, the division itself does not matter to some Irish-Americans, but it does arouse strong feelings in others. The division is not an ascriptive one: Irish-Americans cannot tell by physical appearance who is Catholic and who is Protestant; yet for a proportion of Irish Catholics the knowledge that another person is Protestant would cause them to deny an ethnic link with that person. American Irish Protestants moving from a situation where the split does not matter to one where it does may in fact change their self-identification.

In addition to changes in self-identification owing to changes in the political *significance* of various categories, actual political *changes* can lead to changing self-identification. When boundaries change as the result of wars or conquest, the ethnic identifications of individuals can change too. Joseph Bram cites cases where individuals changed their ethnic identity in midstream because of such political changes. For example: "When at the end of the first World War, Lithuania and Latvia became sovereign independent republics, a surprising number of individuals formerly known as Russians or Poles had rediscovered their Lithuanian or Latvian origin" (1965, 247).

Another situation in which the political significance and connotations of the categories themselves influence self-identification is in the relationship between local and national identities. It has been shown, for instance, that immigrants from Italy to the United States had no sense of themselves as Italians, but rather identified with the locality they were from. The usual expectation is of a movement in the United States toward redefining people as members of wider ethnic groups, deemphasizing previous local identifications. In the case of Maria Reggio, the opposite occurred owing to Maria's understanding of the political and social significance of the ethnic categories themselves. Maria changed her self-identification quite consciously at a point in her life when she realized the connotations associated with the labels "Sicilian" and "Italian." In my interview with her, Maria insisted that she was Sicilian, not Italian. She stated that she would answer Sicilian on her census form and that Sicilian is the ancestry she tells her children about. However, it was not always that way. Growing up in Monterey, she thought of herself as Italian. After she married (a Portuguese man), however, she "discovered" that she was not Italian:

> I am Sicilian really. My folks are from Sicily, and as I was growing up, I thought I was Italian. But I found out later after we were married that I was not. I met this friend of my husband and she said, "Gee, Greg tells my

husband that you are Italian," and I said, "Yes, I am." She said, "Where are you from?" I said that my parents were born in Sicily. She said, "You are not Italian, you are Sicilian." So from then on, I am Sicilian.

Q: Was she Sicilian?

A: Oh, no, she was Italian. Italians do not consider Sicilians Italian. It's like some people say there is as much difference as between Mexicans and Spanish. I did not know that. Sicilians, I guess, are not as rich, not as good from the Italians' point of view. So I am Sicilian, but we did speak Italian. Sicilian has a different slang. It is not as pure as the Italian language.

A chance encounter thus changed Maria's self-identification. Instead of trying to assert her identity as an Italian—which she perceived as a more socially accepted or respected ethnicity—she insisted on emphasizing her Sicilian background.

Of course, all of these rankings compare groups of European origin, which for the most part no longer experience overt discrimination or hostility in the United States. The elements to consider are quite different when one is balancing an ancestry of European origin with a non-European one, where the consequences of a particular identity can be quite serious. An example of this difference is Janet Albert Parro's dilemma about how to label her children. When I interviewed her she was worried about how to characterize her children's ethnicity. Her husband is Spanish and Irish. The forms she has to fill out for school ask about whether the children are Hispanic, and it worries her that there is no distinction made between Mexican-American and Spanish. She is aware that it does not make much difference whether she labels her children Irish or Italian, but that mentioning Spanish ancestry could have ramifications later on. She took the occasion of my interview with her to ask whether putting "Spanish" down on the census form would make her children "Mexican."

A combination of ancestries also raised the issue of social acceptability in the Binet family. During my interview with her, Helen Binet, a 56-year-old salesperson, described her grandfather as German. Later, when I asked about attitudes about other ethnicities, she made a point of telling me that her family had "very old family friends on her father's side who were Jewish" and so she "had no positive or negative feelings about Jews either way." Yet in an interview with her 29-year-old daughter, Terry, a veterinarian, I learned that it was Helen's grandfather who had been Jewish, and that Helen's father had been brought up as a Jew. Terry was uncertain whether her grandfather had later converted to Catholicism. She told me that she had been told this by her father, but that her mother never talked about it. When Terry had learned as a young girl that she had Jewish ancestors, she had thought it was exciting and told all of her friends at school. Then her father had a talk with her and told her that this was not something she should talk about with people outside the family. In fact, it is a family secret that is not discussed openly by family members.

In contrast to families for whom there seem to be positive benefits in enhancing an ethnic identity—for example, by calling themselves Irish, Italian, or Polish—the Binets and the Parros are aware that there are negative social costs associated respectively with labeling children Jewish or Hispanic. In the next chapter we shall look at the structural or social consequences of claiming an identity as an American of European origin and compare them with those felt by Americans of non-European origin.

In the preceding pages we have seen case after case of people sorting and sifting among ethnic categories for their own identities and to decide about the identities of others. It is clear that for most of them ethnicity is not a very big part of their lives. But neither is it something that they give no thought or notice to. It is common in ordinary interactions for people to guess others' backgrounds based on surnames or physical appearance and to be asked by others about their own. Increasingly, though, intermarriage and the ethnic mixtures it brings about make generalizations based on surnames or physical appearance less and less reliable. As that happens, people have more and more latitude about how to self-identify and whether to do so in ethnic terms. Ethnicity is increasingly a matter of personal preference.

It is difficult to examine the choices that these people make in the process of ethnic identification without also examining the content of that identification. We have now seen that for many of my respondents ethnic identification involved a balancing of ethnicity X against ethnicity Y, to determine whether to label oneself X or Y or XY or neither. But what does it mean to be X? How does it influence an individual's life? How does one learn to be X as opposed to Y? It is to this question, to the question of the content of white ethnic identification, that I turn in the next chapters.

CHAPTER 4

Class, Neighborhood, and Ethnicity

What is the meaning of ethnicity for mobile suburban populations of later-generation white ethnics? The fact that ethnic identification is increasingly voluntary does not mean that it lacks meaning or that it will necessarily disappear quickly with the passage of time. My respondents felt that having an ethnicity was, if not essential to their self-identity, a valuable and worthwhile attribute. As we have seen, in most cases of mixed ethnic backgrounds, individuals choose one or two ethnicities to identify with.

While the choices my respondents made about which ancestry to identify with are indeed reminiscent of shopping in a dime store (as Stein and Hill [1977] characterize it), it is not the case that ethnicity is as trivial to them as shopping for a trinket. There is an appreciation of the affective tie to ethnicity that makes it a valuable and appreciated aspect of people's lives. As Irving Howe argues:

> We are all aware that our ties with the European past grow increasingly feeble. Yet we feel uneasy before the prospect of becoming *just Americans* [emphasis added]. We feel uneasy before the prospect of becoming as undistinguishable from one another as our motel rooms are, or as flavorless and mass produced as the bread many of us eat. (Howe 1977, 18)

The twin components of this symbolic ethnicity—that it is in a sense superficial, intermittent, and does not interfere with day-to-day life, while simultaneously representing a source of pleasure and meaning that many of my respondents invest considerable energy in maintaining and perpetuating—is illustrated in the case of Susan Badovich. She reported at the beginning of the interview that she was a third-generation Slovenian. All four of her grandparents emigrated from Yugoslavia to a mining town in Colorado, where her parents grew up. The town was primarily Slovenian. Though Susan was raised in a suburb of San Francisco, where the only other Slovenians she knew were relatives who had also emigrated to San Francisco, she has managed to maintain a very strong tie to her background. She described a number of cultural traditions that she follows with her husband, who is not Slovenian, and her son. These include eating special foods at Christmas and Easter, bringing food to have it blessed by the parish priest, following certain rituals her grandmother taught her, and leaving shoes out on Saint Nicholas's Day and filling them with candy. She attends Slovenian concerts when she can and has taken courses in Slavic history. Yet when she described the ethnic identification of her adopted son, Susan showed that her understanding of ethnicity was in many ways symbolic:

Q: What would you answer on the census form for your son?

A: My son is adopted. He is Irish, Austrian, and English.

Q: Will you bring him up with a special knowledge of his ancestry?

A: I don't know. My husband and I were just talking about this, because I never celebrate Saint Patrick's Day, because I am proud I don't have any Irish in me. But my husband said, "You know, James is half Irish," and I said, "Oh, God, I really feel like I should celebrate Saint Patrick's Day more than I have." I had a friend who went to Germany and I had her bring him back a pair of lederhosen, these little Austrian pants, for the Austrian part of him, and I hope to instill in him some pride in his ethnic background.

Q: Would you ever consider calling him Slovenian?

A: Oh, I never would have said that. He is not. He doesn't look Slovenian. He looks like a little Aryan youth.

Q: What about your husband's ethnicity?

A: He would have answered Russian Jew and English and Scottish on the census form. He really likes his Russian Jew part. We have a mezuzah on the front door. He converted to Catholicism when he married me. He grew up with his mother and she was Baptist, so he was kind of raised in that tradition. But he likes his Russian Jew part more, he feels closer to being Catholic and that part goes together more. They are kind of similar.

Q: How do you know what ancestry your son is?

A: Because we adopted him independently and we met with his birth parents and so we kind of got firsthand what his background was. Oh, also I should mention that my son is one quarter Native American. On top of that.

Q: So as he grows up you are going to try and tell him about his ancestries and what they are?

A: I don't know how we are going to do that. I think we will probably celebrate Saint Patrick's Day and get a book of Irish fairy tales or that kind of thing. Because well, I have been thinking about this stuff. What if he were my age and filling out the census? I really want him to know as much as he is able so he could have something to answer about it.

This mother is not too worried that her son will have any confusion about his ethnic ancestry. She and her husband think they know which symbols are the appropriate ones for an Irish or an Austrian child and they intend to invoke them to raise their child so that he has a particular ethnic identification. As Susan's experience suggests, in order to consider oneself a member of a particular ethnic group all one has to do is to learn the appropriate symbols. The cultural practices and deep feelings of attachment to a particular ethnicity are in a sense superfluous. The idea of her husband liking a Russian Jewish side of himself above an English-Scottish one also highlights the optional character of symbolic ethnicity. In describing this phenomenon Talcott Parsons (1975) stresses that such ethnicity involves a social contract—membership in an ethnic group is essentially voluntary and provides benefits to those who choose to join.

For my respondents, having an ethnic identity was for the most part something that brought pleasure to the individual. Rather than being a handicap to full participation in American society, it was seen as giving one a feeling of community and special status as an interesting or unique individual. This symbolic ethnicity makes no claims or demands on individuals whatsoever. In fact these ethnic groups never have to meet in any meaningful sense, unless you call a Saint Patrick's Day parade a meeting, and yet there is a collectivity with which one can identify and feel a part of in an individualistic and often atomistic society. As illustrated in the previous chapter, my respondents spoke of getting a warm feeling when they met someone else with a surname they recognized as one of their own, even if in fact each of them is only one-eighth of that ethnicity and they share little knowledge of cultural attributes or social conventions that can be traced back to their ethnic origin.

This may partly explain the energy that many respondents invested in maintaining something constantly undermined by structural forces such as intermarriage. Thus Susan Badovich's symbolic understanding of ethnicity would seem to show its unimportance to her, and yet her obvious care and concern with providing even a symbolic ethnicity for her adopted son shows the value she attaches to this ethnic identity.

But what about the content of this ethnic identification? The fact that people are able to respond to a census question on ancestry with an answer other than "American" or "Don't Know" hardly says much about the effect of that ancestry on their lives. Ethnicity is a variable, with a range of meanings attached to it. Some people who answered the census question were merely giving the name of the country that one of their ancestors came from. They perceived no effect on themselves at all and made no conscious identification with other people on the basis of a common ethnic heritage. Others, no doubt, felt quite a strong attachment to the ethnic group. They actively maintained various aspects of their ethnic culture and believed that their ethnic background had a significant influence on their day-to-day lives. A variety of people exhibited a combination of both of these tendencies.

Ascertaining the meaning and effects of ethnicity among later-generation white ethnics is difficult because we can only discern those aspects of ethnicity that a respondent consciously acknowledges, and cannot figure out the ways in which ethnicity might unconsciously affect them. For instance, the identification of fourth-generation English-Americans with one another and with any kind of English political aims or overt cultural practices is virtually nonexistent. The only ethnic identification among them might stem from the fact that someone once told them that their ancestors had come from England in the seventeenth century. A study of individuals such as these would be more revealing if they said that their English ancestry did not matter and yet the researcher somehow found that they were more likely to be emotionally repressed, stress individuality, live in the South, and move away from home at younger ages than people from other ethnic heritages. In that case their ethnicity would in fact be having a noticeable effect on their lives, but it would be operating in ways that were not conscious in the individual. So interviewing is not necessarily conclusive regarding the total effect of ethnicity on the respondents. Even if interviews did not find people acknowledging any ethnicity, it might in fact influence their lives.

The approach taken in this book, then, only identifies behavior, traits, and practices that the individual consciously identifies as ethnic. This may indeed miss behavior and characteristics of individuals that are rooted in ethnic culture and that distinguish Italian-Americans from say, English-Americans. Andrew Greeley (1974, 32) states that much of what is ethnic about a person may be hidden from his/her own consciousness. Greeley and McCready (1975) ingeniously test this proposition by deriving particular social psychological traits and attitudes from ethnographic accounts of Italians in Italy and Irish in Ireland and then seeing whether Italian-Americans and Irish-Americans differ in the hypothesized directions. They find that the religio-ethnic group the individual self-identifies with does correlate strongly with a set of social psychological traits that vary by ethnic group and are related to patterns of behavior and beliefs rooted in the immigrant culture of the root groups. To measure the unconscious manifestations of ethnicity, one would need to observe people at close quarters in a participant-observation study or survey social psychological traits as Greeley has done.

So because an Irish-American respondent claims not to know how the Irish differ from Poles does not necessarily mean that the person in question does not differ from Polish-Americans in some way that reflects true ethnic difference, and I do not want to make that claim here. By asking my respondents to describe the characteristics of their ethnic group, I was asking about those characteristics that they were aware of and perhaps missing some "authentic ethnicity" that they were unaware of. However, I want to report the manner in which my respondents practiced and thought about their ethnicity—both because of the implications of that way of thinking, described in chapter 7, and because of the increasing importance of conscious choice in ethnic identification, described above. To the extent that individuals are increasingly of mixed backgrounds and increasingly have more latitude in how they identify themselves, the conscious meanings they attach to different ethnicities and the degree of importance they give to those meanings become more significant.

In this chapter I describe how my respondents saw their relative affluence and opportunity and the state of discrimination against them, their degree of residential isolation, and their perceptions of and levels of intermarriage.

PERCEPTIONS OF DISCRIMINATION

Sociological studies show that in the past fifty years there has been a sharp decline in the difference among white ethnic groups in socioeconomic attainment.[1] There has been a virtual elimination of visible differences in the ability of individuals in these groups to turn educational attainment into occupational achievement, implying a reduction or elimination of formal discrimination against them. These changes have taken place over the lifetimes of many of my middle-aged respondents. Although the period in which Irish Catholics and Germans were subject to socioeconomic or social discrimination was long enough ago that most respondents had no experience with it, Italian and Polish respondents were old enough to have experienced discrimination themselves. A logical question, then, is, did my respondents report any discrimination or prejudice now or in the past? The answer, for the most part, is no.

A number of studies done by other researchers reach the same conclusions: there is little experience of discrimination among white ethnics today. In Toronto, Canada, Morton Weinfeld found "relatively little personal experience of discrimination for Slavs, Jews or Italians" (1981, 77), and in a study of Italian-Americans in Bridgeport, Connecticut, by James Crispino 86 percent of respondents "reported never having experienced discrimination in housing, getting a job or being promoted" (1980, 118). Respondents whose occupational settings involved large bureaucratic structures were most likely to report discrimination. Micaela di Leonardo similarly found that most of her California Italian-American respondents reported never having experienced discrimination (1984, 159–60).[2] Finally, Colleen Leahy Johnson reports that in her formal interviews respondents rarely discussed prejudice in detail when they were asked directly about it, even with Italian interviewers. Yet incidents were relayed to the interviewers:

> Those incidents reported were the more subtle forms of discrimination—such as an unfriendly reception when one moved into a new neighborhood. Some executives in local businesses concluded that being Italian excluded them from the upper echelons of management, some children were exposed to ethnic epithets at school. (Johnson 1985, 41)

1. See Greeley 1971 and 1976, Hirschman 1983, Yetman 1985 and Neidert and Farley 1985 for discussion of the remarkable socioeconomic progress of the descendants of European immigrants. Alba and Moore 1982 and Pavalko 1980 describe some of the differences among European groups that still exist—particularly evidence of discrimination against Catholics and Jews in the national elite and in top corporations.

2. Later in her interviewing, however, some respondents did start to remember incidents.

My respondents reacted to my questions about prejudice and discrimination in much the same way as the respondents in these other studies. The overwhelming majority reported no prejudice or discrimination on account of their ethnicity. In fact, several women interpreted my question as being about whether they had ever felt discrimination "as women," and answered accordingly. Only three respondents reported direct discrimination. Tom Scotto reported that he had left the telephone company to go into business for himself after being told he could never move into management because he was Italian. When he was passed over for promotion twice, he decided ethnic discrimination was the reason, and he quit and opened his own iron workshop. Now, his ethnicity is a help rather than a hindrance, because it gives him "something to kid about and talk about with the customers when they come in." Maria Reggio reported more indirect discrimination:

Q: Have you ever felt any personal discrimination or hostility?

A: Nothing that I can pinpoint like happening twenty times. But sometimes people just look down, like they would on a Mexican. They said, "Oh, you are Italian." Even Italian. If they found out I was Sicilian, I would really be in serious trouble.

The fact that Maria could not remember a specific incident of discrimination is interesting, because later in the interview she told me the story of her family's relocation during World War II. During the war Maria's family was relocated from the coastline to an inland area for a period of a year and a half because her father was not an American citizen. Whether or not her father was actually a fascist sympathizer, Maria does not seem to interpret this period as an incident of discrimination. However, it could be that she was just too young to remember much or that the incident was so emotionally loaded she did not want to discuss it.[3]

The extent of the discrimination or prejudice felt by younger Italian-Americans had been teasing in school and ethnic jokes, which offended them when they were youngsters. Some Irish-American young people did report that they felt discrimination, not as Irish, but as Catholics. This was reported to occur in the South or when mixing with "blue blood" WASPs. Those who did feel that there was this

---

3. A number of Italians who had not yet become citizens were relocated away from coastal areas during the early years of World War II.

anti-Catholic prejudice could not think of specific incidents or problems; it was just more of a "feeling" they got.

Finally, Betty O'Keefe reported that she had experienced personal discrimination because of her Irish-American background and thought it possible that her children might also be subject to such discrimination:

> When I was in high school my maiden name was Tynan. This was 1940. I was dating some boys from school and two different times when the parents found out I was an Irish Catholic, they told him he couldn't go out with me. The Protestants were like that. One guy's father was a stockbroker—very successful. The other boy's father was a lawyer. One of his brothers later married someone named O'Flannery and I was so thrilled. I said I hope your mother is turning in her grave. So I am very happy that my children have the name O'Keefe. So that people know right away what their background is. I think it is better. They would never be put in the position I was in.
>
> Q: Do you think something like that could happen now?
>
> A: I don't think as openly. But I think it is definitely still there. You are not as bad as a black, but you are not Protestant. You are not Jewish either, which would be worse, but still you are not of their church.

But most of my sample had no such direct experience with any type of prejudice or discrimination because of their ethnicity. Many of them were aware of a history of discrimination or prejudice against their groups, but for the most part it was either something they had learned in school or something they "supposed their ancestors felt." For instance, some people claimed that their grandparents or great-grandparents "must have experienced some problems somewhere," because their last names had been changed at some point in the past. But for these suburban ethnics, ethnicity is not perceived as a handicap in the society at large.

RESIDENTIAL SEGREGATION

A second indicator of ethnic group assimilation/segregation identified by sociologists is the degree of residential segregation. This has long been used as an indicator of assimilation of ethnic groups into the wider society. As Stanley Lieberson summarizes it, "Segregation influences a wide variety of social phenomena such as intermarriage, linguistic assimilation, and even the maintenance of a group's distinctive occupational composition" (1980, 253).

The concern with the degree of residential segregation of an ethnic group dates back to the assimilation theories of the founders of the Chicago school, Robert Park and Ernest W. Burgess (1925). Their model of ethnic succession had as its cornerstone the idea that as generations in the United States progressed, the children and grand-children of immigrants would no longer need the "total environment" of the ethnic ghetto to cope with the stresses of industrial life and immigration. They would then move further away from the central business district and become more integrated into the wider society and other ethnic groups. Decades of empirical research on this issue have generally supported this predicted decline in residential segregation for white European immigrants and their descendants, but have not found it to be true for non-white groups (Hirschman 1983).

Studies of residential segregation of white ethnic groups conducted in the twentieth century tell a story of declining residential segregation accompanying socioeconomic achievement and increases in status. These studies identify high degrees of ethnic residential segregation for the "new" (at that time) European immigrants from southern, central, and eastern European countries, which declined over time (Lieberson 1980, 270; Guest and Weed 1976). These changes within cities have coincided with the growth in suburbanization of the population. Catholic white ethnic groups are increasingly becoming suburbanized along with the rest of the country (Alba 1976, 1985b, 88).

The move to the suburbs of the increasingly assimilated ethnic group members is hypothesized to further reduce the salience of ethnicity and the ties to the ethnic group, because it is believed that the suburbs will act as great melting pots, exposing the white ethnics to heterogeneous social networks and institutions and markets not dominated by their own ethnic group (Cohen 1977, 998). In part I chose to interview suburban Catholics because suburbanization has been hypothesized to reduce ethnic ties. In the interviews I asked about some of the ways in which this suburbanization and movement away from ethnic neighborhoods had been experienced by the respondents in my sample.

I asked my respondents how they would characterize the neighborhood they lived in, and what kind of neighborhood they had grown up in. The differences between the replies of most of the older, middle-aged respondents about their current living situations and the ones they had grown up in were quite striking. Many of them reported growing up in an environment in which white ethnic groups and the differences between them were very important. This was contrasted with the perception that their Silicon Valley or Philadelphia Main Line suburb was not the same. Ethnic differences were still important, but those most respondents referred to were among Asians, Hispanics, blacks, and whites.

In response to the questions of what their neighborhoods had been like when they were growing up, many middle-aged respondents from cities in the East and Midwest as well as from San Francisco remembered a distinct ethnic flavor. Many of them mapped the city in terms of parishes. Bonnie Ostrowski described Chicago:

> Some of the other people in my neighborhood were German and there was quite a large contingency of Lithuanian people in our area. In this small area there were four major Catholic churches...There were two Polish parishes and then Saint Joseph's and Saint Anne's. They were what I would call international. They had English, Irish, French.

Some of the middle-aged respondents I interviewed were not from central city areas, but had grown up in older suburbs. However, they, too, remembered ethnic neighborhoods in the suburbs. Anne Gold:

> Cleveland is basically an ethnic city. We lived in the suburbs and our suburb was mostly Polish, with some Hungarians, and some Italians, and of course the Irish. There were no blacks in our particular suburb, but I dealt with them all of the time in Cleveland. It was segregated for everyone. You had the Hungarians over here, and the Italians over there, etc.

The general tone with which these respondents remembered the ethnic neighborhoods was very positive. Most described tightly knit communities, evoking a warm, integrated scene. Sean O'Brien:

> There were a few non-Irish in my neighborhood, and they were Italian. But it was mostly Irish Catholic. I could make a few phone calls and I could muster up about thirty or forty Irish and about one or two Italians. There were about thirty of us who used to run around and play baseball and we used to have one token Italian. We did not associate with others. We were kind of clannish. All the Irish guys, the Murphys, the O'Neals, the Corbetts, the Hearns, we all ran around together and drank beer. We used to drink beer in one bar up the corner and all the guys would drink in that bar, and one block away all the fathers would drink in another bar, and if you were looking for your father, just go up a block. That is the way it was.

In contrast to the middle-aged respondents who had lived in ethnic neighborhoods when they were growing up, a number of the young adults I interviewed had spent their lives in the suburbs, which were not perceived by them as being ethnic in any way. When asked to describe the ethnic makeup of their neighborhoods, they denied that they had any ethnic flavor at all, frequently categorizing the residents simply as white. "Growing up in a small-town suburb, everyone's ethnicity seems pretty much the same," as Patrick O'Connor put it.

The older generation shared this perception of their current neighborhood not being characterized by any particular white ethnic group. Anne Gold's response was typical:

Q: Is the neighborhood you live in now characterized by any particular ethnic group?

A: I have absolutely no idea. We have lived here eighteen years. They have an Irish name over there [points to next-door neighbor], but I don't know anything else.

I asked my respondents whether they thought they were missing something by not living in an ethnic neighborhood. Although people did speak fondly of remembered ethnic neighborhoods, most replied that they were perfectly happy with the way their neighborhood was. Some of the younger respondents who had spent their whole lives in the suburbs, however, reported that they did think they were lacking some type of "ethnic experience." Patricia Quinn:

Sometimes I think I am missing something. My mom and I went to Boston a couple of years ago and we went through this Italian neighborhood and they were all setting up for this carnival and it was neat. You do get a sense of missing that, a strong neighborhood identity. And I really don't have a strong neighborhood identity. I don't even know all of my neighbors.

In these cases, the ethnic neighborhood is viewed as an experience that might be enriching or rewarding and that one has missed out on by living in a white suburb. Some people solve this problem by "commuting" to the ethnic neighborhood when they desire some ethnic experience. Rose Scotto reports that she and her husband go to North Beach (the Italian neighborhood in San Francisco) for food and the 11 A.M. Mass on Sundays, which is said in Italian.

Dan Burke also thought he had the best of all worlds. He could live in his suburban home and have a community without ethnicity being prominent, and yet he was close to San Francisco. So when he wanted heterogeneity, he could just go visit it:

If it was just Silicon Valley or Sacramento or something, it would be bad. San Francisco is very diverse ethnically and that is so close and I think we have benefited from that. Because of the proximity I can go to North Beach or to Chinatown whenever I want.

Most of my respondents either fondly remembered an ethnic neighborhood of their youth or, having grown up in the suburbs, had an image of an ethnic neighborhood that was warm and provided community. The sentiment was that ethnic neighborhoods don't truly exist anymore, but that while they did they were sources of warmth and support.

Most respondents were not aware of ethnic differences in their neighborhood, but many were very aware of racial or minority groups and their presence or absence in the neighborhood. This also echoes the results of residential segregation studies, which show that neighborhoods are now defined by racial as opposed to ethnic lines.

In the neighborhoods where I interviewed, there were so few blacks that people did not comment much on them. In the California neighborhood the non-whites who were present were mostly Asians. The real change in the neighborhood that everyone noticed was the influx of Asians. Many of the respondents were worried about the number of Asians moving into the neighborhood. They perceived them as being very different from white people. Robert Albert:

> They [the Vietnamese] are starting to be clannish like that, living in certain areas, the other Asians too, and the people who came over from Cuba. I don't think that there are any ethnic neighborhoods anymore. People just move in and move out. Especially down here on the peninsula. But the Asians keep to themselves.

Barbara Richter saw the same trend:

> I would say that now there has just been such an influx of all kinds of foreign people. There are so many Indians and Pakistanis and lots of Orientals...And they are different. I am just talking in our neighborhood. They don't neighbor like Caucasian people do.

Many people in the California sample mentioned the large numbers of Vietnamese entering the area and, like Barbara Richter, were able to tell me which houses had been sold to Asians in the recent past. People were also very aware of which neighborhoods and areas had Mexican-American residents.[4]

4. The suburban Philadelphia sample did not describe any non-whites in their parish area, although some people did say that they were worried that some might someday move in.

INTERMARRIAGE

Besides the perception of discrimination and the degree of residential segregation, a third and very important indicator of the degree of ethnic assimilation is intermarriage. Social scientists have been interested in documenting and studying the levels of intermarriage for several important reasons. First, intermarriage is important because of the significance of the family as the primary institution of socialization of children. If the husband and wife are not from the same ethnic group, it is assumed that the children's ethnic socialization will not be as strong as it would be if both parents were from the same group. As a result it seems reasonable that the perpetuation of ethnic identification among the children is not as assured when there are high levels of intermarriage. "A homogeneous nuclear family, along with a homogeneous extended family, is more able and likely to pass on to offspring the ethnic feelings, identification, culture, and values that will help perpetuate the group," as Lieberson and Waters (1988, 165) note.

While intermarriage alone does not mean that the children will not strongly identify with one or other parent's ethnic ancestry (as we have seen in previous chapters), it does lead to a possible dilution of ethnic identification within the family.

Second, there is evidence that intermarriage lessens the ethnic behavior and attachments of the husband or wife who marries out of the ethnic group. A primary finding of previous research is that intermarriage directly affects the social network of the husband and wife, and indirectly affects the extended family, making it more heterogeneous (Johnson 1985; Abramson 1971).

A third reason to study this subject is that in addition to being an agent of change in itself, intermarriage is also quite a good indicator of changes in the nature and perception of ethnic boundaries. If boundaries become less salient to people, it is likely that you will see an increase in the level and trend of marriage across these boundaries.

Finally, the consequences of intermarriage for the marriage itself are a subject of interest. Does the act of marrying someone from a different ethnic, religious or racial background lead to problems in the marriage? Do these marriages need special attention from mental health practitioners (McGoldrick 1982, 2)? Do they end in divorce more often than other marriages, or are they just culturally richer, embodying blends of different cultures that are beneficial for the parties involved?

Information on what constitutes an in- or out-marriage is not always discernible from official statistics. The boundaries used by the statisticians may not be the same as the social boundaries people observe. For instance, two people of Italian descent who marry would be considered an in-marriage in terms of the Italian ethnic group by most survey researchers today. However there was a time when the distinction between a northern and southern Italian would have made a marriage between these two people a marriage across ethnic boundaries. There were distinctions among Jews in the United States that made some people consider a marriage between a Russian Jew and a German Jew an out-marriage as recently as twenty years ago (Friedman 1982, 514). One of the questions I am concerned with here is the fit between these two types of boundaries. What is an "out-marriage" or an "in-marriage" for my respondents, and how do they learn the definitions of these social boundaries? What are the salient boundaries in terms of who is considered a good or suitable marriage partner? Have these boundaries been changing? How do perceptions and boundaries on this issue change?

The most striking evidence in all accounts of intermarriage in the United States concerns the very low levels of intermarriage between blacks and whites. Ninety-nine percent of American-born black women in their first marriage have mates who are also black (Lieberson and Waters 1988). Although there are no longer any official barriers to black-white intermarriage in the United States (until 1967, when they were declared unconstitutional, nineteen states had laws prohibiting racial intermarriage [McGoldrick 1982, 21]), the unofficial boundaries clearly remain very strong.

The 1980 census data allow us to look at the intermarriage of later-generation white ethnics and at the behavior of people of mixed ancestry. Lieberson and Waters (1988) analyzes these data and describes the major trends of intermarriage in the United States today. Using cohort changes to infer longitudinal change, we concluded that while endogamy among white ethnic groups is declining, sometimes rapidly for more recent groups, there is still a level of endogamy far in excess of what one would expect on the basis of chance alone. This is true even for people who are themselves the product of mixed marriages. While the tendency to marry someone with the same or overlapping ethnic ancestry is not as strong as for those of single ancestry, even those of mixed ancestry still show a preference for someone who shares one or more of their ancestries.

The evidence on declining rates of in-marriage—especially for the younger cohorts of white ethnic groups—is striking for some of the Catholic groups from which members of my sample come. For example, among Italians, those over 65 years of age are 137 times more likely to be married to another Italian than are non-Italians. However, those aged 25–34 are only 8 times as likely to be. There is thus a sharp drop in the in-marriage tendency of Italians. Yet the younger Italians are still 8 times more likely to be married to another Italian than are non-Italians. For white ethnics, the longer a group has been in the United States and the greater the percentage of its members in later generations, the lower the in-marriage ratios.

These trends are very different from the trends for interracial marriages. The statistics for blacks are striking in comparison. Blacks over the age of 65 have an in-marriage odds ratio of 79,495 to 1, as compared to blacks aged 25–34, who have a ratio of 19,131 to 1. This means that the youngest cohort of blacks are still 19,131 times more likely to marry a black than a white. While there is a decline in in-marriage between these two age cohorts, there is still negligible intermarriage occurring in the United States between blacks and whites.

The evidence on intermarriage across religious lines is not as clear-cut as evidence for racial or ethnic groups. The "triple melting pot" hypothesis described by Will Herbert (1955) has often been used to describe the situation in the Untied States as regards religious intermarriage. The triple melting pot was based on the notion that as ethnic divisions declined, the new divisions in society would be among the three major religious groupings, with Catholic, Protestant, and Jewish pools intermarrying and maintaining boundaries and social distance between the groups.

My interviews on how respondents saw the issue of intermarriage show that the salient boundaries for them were by far racial ones. While they were aware of the ethnicity of mates and potential mates, there did not seem to be too much perception of "crossing a boundary" in marrying someone of a different ethnicity. Religion was a somewhat intermediate obstacle, with a fair number of people asserting that marriage outside of their religion was a major step.

I asked my respondents about how their parents felt or would have felt about them dating or marrying someone of a different ethnicity, religion, or race. The answers to these questions reflect the wider changes and trends in marriage patterns just described. Middle-aged respondents whose parents were either first-generation or second-generation ethnics did recall that their parents wanted them to marry within their ethnic group. Tales of parents being upset about an out-marriage are also among the most common "family stories" passed down from generation to generation. Quite a few respondents told stories of parents or grandparents who were ostracized for not marrying a fellow ethnic. However, most respondents of the fourth and later generations received no direct messages about marrying within their own ethnic group, although some did report indirect signals about this.

Religion was far more important to the parents of all of my respondents, although there were still some who reported that it made no difference. Race was universally an issue, and marriage across racial barriers was not the subject of subtle clues or indirect messages. Most parents made it very clear to their children that they were not to marry a non-white.

Most of the people who said that their parents directly told them to date someone from the same ethnic group were either the children of immigrants or the third generation in a heavily ethnic family. Many of them were currently in-married, but they saw this more as a matter of "having found the right person," who happened to be Irish or Polish or German, rather than it being the result of listening to parental advice. In fact, many respondents made a point of telling me about siblings who had in-married and subsequently got divorced. This evidence was cited to show me that their parents were wrong: being from the same ethnic group does not necessarily lead to a happier marriage. Mary McGowan, who did marry an Irishman, told how her parents' insistence on dating only Irish boys was quite ironic:

> My father thought the Irish were the greatest. In fact, he used to say, "If you are not Irish Catholic, then you are no good." Honest to God, he believed that. It was important for them that I date Irish boys. I dated one little fellow who had come right from Ireland and that made them so happy. This fellow would come to the house and, oh, God, my parents thought it was great. But they didn't know! He was bad! He had roaming hands and rushing fingers. I didn't like that. I said, "Tim, keep your hands to yourself." And I didn't want to go out with him anymore. I didn't have the heart to tell my parents why, they thought he was so great.

Maria Reggio, who married a Portuguese man, reported that her parents had definitely pushed her to date other Italians, although she says they were being open-minded by not expecting that she date only southern Italians: "They would have liked to have kept the Italian blood, so to speak." Two of her siblings had married Italians, not Sicilians, and then later divorced. Maria hastily told me that it was not because they were Italian that they divorced. Yet when I asked her about whether she would prefer it if her children married Italians (her children are half Portuguese), she answered affirmatively:

> Sure, I hope they marry someone from the same ethnic group. But it is not that big a push. The only reason that I do like to see it is because their backgrounds are so much more compatible. It is not a drastic change. My niece came over the other day and she is the same age as my children, nineteen or twenty, and she is going with an Italian boy and they are so compatible. You can see it in the way they talk. It is like belonging to a club. They talk the same because their mothers talk the same. Not that any other man or any other boy would not be OK. It seems like it is a little easier. They know what an Italian father is like and that's all.

She reported that her marriage with her Portuguese husband worked so well because Italians and Portuguese were so much alike—they both valued "family" (more on this in chapter 6).

It is not only through direct messages that parents tell children to marry or date within their own religion, but also through indirect positive approval. Patrick O'Connor, a fifth-generation Irish-American, was sure his parents would secretly be overjoyed if he were to have an Irish girlfriend:

> They are so careful not to tell me to date Irish girls, that it is always there. My brothers and I have all dated non-Irish people, so that it is a big joke in the family. My parents would not get upset if I got serious about a non-Irish girl...They would prefer a Catholic for sure, but they would sort of feel like a tradition was being continued if I married an Irish person. I would not say they would feel happier. It is not that cut-and-dry. I want to give them credit. They are not that prejudiced. But at the same time I am aware of it. I think my brothers probably are too.

Carol Davis also reported that her parents were secretly happy when someone in her family chose another Irish person:

> Q: Did your parents want you to date other Irish?
>
> A: It was never really discussed, although my father was happy that John had the Irish in him, or I guess he was happy that he wasn't Italian. Something like that. Or black. That would have really flipped him out. He would have died. So they don't really say much, but

> when someone marries or dates someone that has a lot of Irish blood, they are real happy about it. It is like an added bonus, but it is not really discussed until after the fact. They are not big on Italians for some reason.

Some of my respondents in their twenties and thirties actually laughed at the question of whether they wanted to marry someone from the same ethnic group. "Do people really say yes to these questions?" one woman asked incredulously. In fact, only one person did admit that she had thought she would want to marry someone of the same ethnic group, "to keep the blood line pure." However, she had married twice already, and neither person was a fellow ethnic. Of course, part of the reason that many parents do not advise their children to marry within their ethnic groups is that they themselves have already intermarried. Many people responded to my question about this with the statement that because they had intermarried, they certainly couldn't tell their children not to do it.

While the messages to offspring about marrying a fellow ethnic are subtle and most people are sure that not much would happen if they did not follow such advice, the messages about interreligious marriage that people reported getting from their parents were much clearer. Very few people reported that their parents were not opposed to interreligious marriages. Christine O'Brien:

> I think the big thing was Catholic. It was narrow. Stick to the Catholic, don't get into trouble. Catholic was the big thing. But it was never the dominant thing that he was Italian or Irish. The Catholic thing we were taught in school too, and so it was carried through at home as well as school.

People were actually more likely to admit that they themselves agreed with their parents' wishes that they marry another Catholic. It seemed less socially unacceptable than saying that they agreed with their parents' admonitions to marry within their ethnic group. (Of course, this finding may be strongly influenced by the special nature of my sample—active Roman Catholics.) Marrying within your religion was not seen as stemming from prejudice, but from a sound weighing of all of the things that could go wrong in a marriage.

Janet Albert Parro admitted that it was important for her parents that their kids marry Catholic. She thought it became even more important because her older brother's first marriage had been to a non-Catholic and ended in divorce. However, she admitted that mar-

rying Catholic was a concern for her even if it was not high on her list
of priorities:

> If I were looking for a husband now, if something happened, and I had to
> date again, I would not say, "You have to be Catholic or I am not
> interested." It just happened when my husband and I met that he was
> Catholic. It was nice. Because there can be problems. It makes it easier. If I
> had to go out and search again, I would not make it a priority, but it does
> make it easier, especially in terms of raising your children.

Her father, Robert, reported having had stronger feelings on the
subject as a young man: "It was an issue for me. I felt I should marry
within my religion. I did date girls of different religions, but it was
afterwards when you really got serious, and then you weigh all of the
different factors. You feel that you would have something more in
common if the two of you share religious beliefs." When something
goes wrong in an interfaith marriage, many people chalk it up to that.
Christine O'Brien: "My mother is saying now that all Jews are no
good because my sister married a Jewish boy and now they are getting
divorced, and now all of a sudden everyone is OK as long as he is not
Jewish."

The escalation from feelings about marrying within one's ethnicity
to marrying within one's religion and to within one's race was almost
universal. In general, people felt very strongly about marrying within
one's race. This, too, was a generational phenomenon; the younger
people felt more embarrassed about parental advice about not marrying across the color line. Pete Scotto, a 20-year-old college student,
reported the messages his father gave him:

> Outside of my race would be the worst in their eyes. I remember our
> conversations of that type would begin with the statement that black
> people could never marry white people. We would get all of these analo-
> gies that I can't really think of right now. They are really embarrassing. It
> was unnatural. He would invariably wind up saying that black and white
> was impossible. And Italian and Irish was really common but that Italian
> and Italian was the best.

While parents give subtle messages about ethnicity or religion,
most messages about race were far from subtle. Joyce Hoffman:

> I always knew that I should not date blacks.
>
> Q: Did [your parents] say that directly to you?
>
> A: Well, they would not let a black person into the house, so that sort of
>   gave me the idea.

Ellen Albert:

> I think that if I had come home with a Mexican I would have gotten a good swift kick.

Megan O'Keefe, a 28-year-old housewife:

> I had a few black friends and sometimes they would visit and my mother used to get very upset. I brought one home with me once, and it happened to be a man and my mother was putting everything away because she thought he was going to steal it. I was so embarrassed.

Joe Williams, a 32-year-old salesman:

> My dad would have died if I had married a black person. He is kind of liberal, but I think he would never have gotten over that. Jewish—that maybe too would have bothered them, but probably not as much.

Crispino (1980, 113) asked his respondents (second- and third-generation Italian-Americans) whether it was important for them to have their children marry endogamously. Only 3 percent said yes for ethnicity, 12 percent said yes for class, and 34 percent said yes for religion. I also found that very few respondents reported that they wanted their children to marry within their ethnic group. Pete Scotto's father, Tom, a second-generation Italian-American was the exception:

> We would prefer our children marry Italians. It is easier if you are from the same background. But we know it won't happen probably. Our kids decide these things for themselves. We just feel it would be easier for them, they would know one another better because they would be from the same background. But it is up to them. We have no right to expect it.

> Q: What about religion?

> A: Once again it is up to them. We just want what is best for them. We think it is even harder to marry outside of the religion. How would you raise the kids? That is the most important question. But this is a decision that the kids make on their own. It is not up to their mother and me. We just want their happiness.

> Q: Does that apply to marrying people from other races?

> A: Absolutely not! [Bangs fist on table.] Race is another story. My children should marry a Caucasian. There is no reason to go outside your own race. It is not right. They have nothing in common with the people from the other races. A Chinese or Japanese or a black person should not marry a Caucasian. There is absolutely no reason to do that. I would object very strongly if my child wanted to do something like that. It is just not the same.

Tom Scotto represents perhaps the most extreme reaction on this issue. Most people were just silently insistent on the issue of race.

Like interreligious marriage, people were much more likely to agree with their parents about interracial dating and marriage or to express extremely prejudiced reactions or feelings directly. Even the most prejudiced people, though, couched their extreme feelings in terms of "how hard it would be for the couple involved," but lurking below the surface were some strong anti-black feelings. Ted Jackson spoke plainly:

> I don't like it. Now when you say interracial, I think black and white. Now if I could use some stereotypes or some slang, it would be easier to speak. I feel that there is black people and there is niggers. And there is Puerto Ricans and there is Spicks. You know where I am coming from? I wouldn't approve of either type marrying a white. Because I see what goes on and it is just too hard. No matter how hard you try to make it work, it might work for two people in the home, but outside the home there is just too many outside influences. They constantly have to feel walked on. People will always be saying things about them that they have to brush off. It has got to wear on these people. A black and a white never. I would never consider it at all.

Rose Peters gave a more "liberal" response:

> I personally don't have anything against it, but I think it is an uncomfortable situation, especially if they have kids and then the child has to decide if they are white or black. I think it is hard for them, but if they want to and they are willing to overcome the obstacles. I would not object to living next door to a family that was interracial.

THE CONSEQUENCES OF INTERMARRIAGE FOR THOSE INVOLVED

In some of the literature on intermarriage there have been suggestions that the different personality styles and cultural expectations that people bring from their ethnic groups would lead to problems in such marriages. For instance, Monica McGoldrick (1982) suggests that Irish-Americans are likely to distance themselves from other people and withdraw when they get upset about something. On the other hand, Italian-Americans are likely to express their emotions forcefully and provoke confrontations. These cultural differences can then lead to misunderstandings among the people involved.

Liz Field did attribute the failure of her first marriage in part to the differences between her English-Welsh-Scottish background and her husband's Italian background. She described the differences she saw between the two families at her own wedding:

> My family is very reserved and doesn't say much about how they are feeling. They are very aloof. They step backwards so as not to offend anybody...His family was very open-hearted and eager to get to know this other family. They were just so happy. Their kids are happy because they are going to get married. And my family was very aloof and reserved and very unwilling to forget their problems. And the other side wasn't. They were different.

The problems people did discuss mostly centered on family acceptance of the spouse who married in. Many families had stories— usually one generation back, but sometimes current—of extreme rejection of an ethnic out-marriage. Suzanne Benson's parents had had a difficult time because of their parents' reaction to an Irish-Italian intermarriage:

> My father's family stopped talking to my mother because she was Irish. And they used to sit around the table and talk in Italian because they knew that she did not understand the language.
>
> Q: Did your father's family eventually come around?
>
> A: No, my father actually stopped talking to them because of it. They'll talk once in a while, but we are not close.

Rose Scotto's sister married an Irishman. Though she told me that she thought the Irish and the Italians were well suited to each other, and that she accepted her brother-in-law and thought he was great because he cooked for them on Saint Patrick's Day, her son Pete told me a different story. Pete Scotto reported that his uncle's Irishness was always discussed, and that he was believed to have a terrible temper and to be hot-headed because he was Irish.

The usual reaction in families that was reported to me was kidding about aspects of the outsider that did not fit the culture they had married into. For Robert Albert, the kidding from his parents came when he first started dating his Irish future wife: "I think my wife did get a few barbs from my grandmother, and my uncle would just kid her. Like they would say to me, 'How come you couldn't find a nice little Italian girl?' But I don't think they were too serious. In fact one time before I met my wife they tried to fix me up with a Greek girl. So they were not too serious." Ellen Albert reported that she had gradually adopted some of her husband's family's Italian traditions: "I wasn't much of a cook, but I learned to cook. I learned to cook Italian from Bob's mother. Like tonight I am going to make cannoli. And I learned to make pizza—not like we buy at Straw Hat; it is a thick dough pizza. That is what his mother made; they call it *pigazza*."

There is often an adjustment pattern evident where the wife marrying into an Italian family undergoes a process of "Italianization." Micaela di Leonardo found such cases in her study of suburban Californian Italian-Americans (1984, 223). Colleen Leahy Johnson (1985, 130) found a similar process of "Italianization" taking place among Italian-Americans in Syracuse, New York.

Rose Peters' grandparents were very insistent that she and her brothers and sisters marry other Italians—even though they were not both Italians themselves, because this process of Italianization was so advanced with her grandmother.

Q: Was it important for your mom's family that she would marry another Italian?

A: Yes, in fact it was a big stink when she married the Irish. And it took my father a few years to prove himself to my grandfather. When I married an Irishman, my grandfather told me I had disappointed him. And my sister married an Italian and when the four of us would visit them her husband was always favored. He could go in the refrigerator without asking. We had to ask permission.

Q: That is interesting since your grandparents were not all Italian. Wasn't your grandmother Lithuanian?

A: Yes. Well, I think my grandfather was the dominant one in the family. For a long time I bet my grandmother even thought that she was Italian. Because she had to learn to speak Italian to communicate with his parents. She had to learn how to cook all the Italian food, and she belonged to the Italian church. So she really went to his way of life.

And Rose mentioned later that the coping mechanism her father adopted to deal with the disapproval of her mother's parents was to become "semi-Italian" himself.

While this may be the result in some heavily ethnic Italian-American families, it was more likely among the people I interviewed for the wife to maintain her ethnic identity (recall Ellen Alberts' pride in her Irish heritage) but to adopt certain aspects of the culture of the spouse's family. A type of cultural syncretism is occurring. In fact, the match between Irish and Italian seems to be producing a very identifiable collectivity. Irish-Italian matches were frequently reported to me as being "a good combination." The children of such marriages were

said to be exceptionally beautiful, and the balancing of the "emotional" Italians and the "reserved" Irish was supposed to produce a
"good mix." The Scottos reported that just before I interviewed them
the parish priest had told them that they should find a nice Irish girl
for their Italian boys because the "excitable" Italians needed "calmer"
Irish to balance them out.

Not everyone saw this as a great match though. Father Pat Stevens,
a 47-year-old Catholic priest, reported that in his family there were a
lot of hard feelings when an aunt or uncle or cousin married outside
of the Irish group. (Father Stevens is Irish and German, but he and his
family identify strongly with their Irish ancestry.) Christine O'Brien
reported that the Irish-Italian mix that characterized her and her
husband's marriage was not warmly received by his family:

> Because I was from an Italian family, that they did not like, and they were
> not broad enough to find out who I was and so they reacted to me. His
> grandmother, in fact, would not come to the wedding because he was
> marrying into my family. And she automatically said no...But I was
> marrying Sean, not them. So it didn't matter. But sure it hurt.

This extreme reaction to ethnic differences was by far the exception to the rule. For the most part, ethnic differences were hardly
noticed, or if they were noticed it was to kid about them or to remark
about some difference between people. This was clear when I asked
people about the ethnicity of those their brothers and sisters had
married. For many, not only was there no family crisis about marrying outside the group, but there was even difficulty in recalling the
spouse's ethnicity.

It is clear that the whites in my sample were not conscious of
negative consequences stemming from their ethnic identities. They
also were not conscious of clear and distinct boundaries separating
white ethnic groups from each other. For the most part, none of them
reported having experienced any discrimination or prejudice. Many
older respondents could remember white ethnic neighborhoods from
their childhood, but the areas they live in now are not characterized
by any particular white ethnic group. The salient geographic boundaries for these white ethnics are the boundaries between whites and
non-whites. These are what define their neighborhoods.

The same was true of intermarriage. Among younger respondents
there was no stated conscious desire to marry a co-ethnic, beyond
fleeting references to "preserving the blood line." The important

messages young people receive from parents and the actions that result (as evidenced by the census data) all point to the importance of racial, and to a lesser extent religious, boundaries in the choice of a marriage partner. Thus the boundaries important to my respondents in terms of quantifiable, structural variables were those that separate black from white, white from Asian, and Jew from Catholic, not Pole from Italian or German from English. But while structural barriers do not exist or are not salient for distinguishing among the ethnic identifications of whites in my sample, other, more cultural, indicators of ethnicity do exist and are indeed meaningful to them. This *cultural* content of ethnicity is the subject of the next chapter.

CHAPTER 5

Cultural Practices

Ethnicity does have meaning for the individuals I interviewed. For the most part, a claim to a certain ancestry given to the Census Bureau is not an empty label. Increasingly, however, the substance attached to that label is constructed by the individual and the family. People have to construct the image of what it means to be Italian or Polish or Irish from the characteristics of their family, what they believe to be ethnic, or from a cultural grab bag of Irish, Polish, or Italian stereotypical traits. A consequence of this construction is that it is difficult for respondents to be sure what constitutes ethnicity as opposed to idiosyncratic family values and practices. The substance of this ethnicity is also selective, intermittent, and symbolic. You can choose those aspects of being Irish that appeal to you and discard those that do not.

The questions I asked about the meaning of ethnicity can be broadly divided into two categories: cultural practices or holidays still adhered to or celebrated by the family that embody "ethnic tradition" and social psychological traits and behavior that make a person "Italian" or "Polish." I shall discuss the first of these, cultural practices, in this chapter, and the social psychological traits in the next.

As many sociologists have predicted and described, much of what my respondents associated with being ethnic is symbolic and intermittent in nature (Gans 1979; Crispino 1980; Alba 1985b; Roche

1984; Weinfeld 1981). In response to my questions about ethnic foods, holidays, and use of language, most respondents talked of the "special occasions" when they did something they thought of as uniquely "ethnic." The fact that these cultural manifestations of ethnicity are somewhat intermittent and consciously maintained, however, does not diminish their importance. In the tract houses of Silicon Valley and the suburban homes of Philadelphia, there is a diversity of distinctive ethnic practices and observations being maintained.

LANGUAGE

Language is one of the first elements of the immigrant culture to disappear over the generations. It is also one of the cultural attributes that has the strongest effect in maintaining solidarity and integration in the ethnic group (Stevens 1985). The rapidity with which fluency in an ancestral language is lost was evident in my sample. Only four out of the sixty people I interviewed were fluent in the language of their ancestors. Three had spoken the language with their parents and the fourth had studied it in school. They all reported that they had become "rusty" since their parents had died, and that they had not taught their own children the language.

The experience of most people in my sample with their ancestral language consisted of remembering their grandparents speaking it or remembering certain phrases or words that they had been taught as children. Rather than being experienced as an integrative link with a wider ethnic community, the vestiges of immigrant European languages are experienced in a very different way by the third and later generations. They have been taught small phrases or words or heard their grandparents, uncles, or aunts speaking when they were children. The language itself is not easily separated in their minds from family traditions, childhood memories, and particular occasions or events.

Many in the third generation in my sample could not speak the language, for example, but could remember being able to understand it when they were young. For many the ethnic language was only spoken between themselves and their grandparents. Rather than functioning as a link between themselves and co-ethnics, the ethnic language was experienced as a private affair—spoken with grandparents or parents only in the home. It came to be understood not as something linking them to a wider collectivity, to a community or an ethnic group, but as a secret language that they only knew when they were quite young and that was only used within the family. Rather than being a link to fellow ethnics for this third generation, the language was thus a link with the remembered past.

Once the link with parents or grandparents was broken, respondents had no easy way or little desire to maintain the language in their present situations. Bonnie Ostrowski grew up speaking Polish with her parents and attended a Polish Catholic grammar school, where she learned to read and write Polish. As she described it, however, she had been steadily losing the ability:

> I never taught my own children, because my husband cannot speak it. Even though his last name sounds Polish, on his father's side there is Polish, but his mom was German, Scots, and Irish, and he didn't speak it at all because he is like a third-generation American. So I never taught my own children. When my parents were still alive, I still spoke it, because they would come out to California two or three times a year. I would also talk to them on the phone twice a month. But my dad has been dead nineteen years and my mom has been dead ten years. I could probably still speak it to someone, but I would probably Americanize a lot of words if I couldn't think of it fast enough...Every once in a while I will teach my youngest daughter, Judy, something that you wouldn't want to have repeated. A silly phrase or a silly name or that type of thing.

John Davis also has "little phrases" that he remembers his mother teaching him when he was a young child:

> I could speak just a couple of words in Czech. I know how to say belly button in Czech.
>
> Q: Did your mother speak Czech?
>
> A: Yes, I think both her parents spoke Czech. Now I am confused whether it was both her parents or grandparents. I think both her grandparents did, but I think her parents did a lot too. So she learned it pretty well, but you know it died out. She didn't use it too much. I remember her saying that her parents used to argue back and forth in Czech. Sometimes I'd teach my son some of these Czech words, just for kidding around.

The words and phrases these people describe are spoken only within the family and often only at certain times or certain places. People therefore learn bits and pieces of the language, and learn to associate it with the things going on in their family when they heard these bits and pieces. Suzanne Benson recalled: "My father...would speak

Italian when he got mad. That is the only time. I remember being scared of it when I was a kid. If you heard some Italian, boy were you in trouble."

Though these "silly phrases" are often all that remains of the language of the immigrants among their grandchildren and great-grandchildren, people trying consciously to maintain or rekindle an ethnic identity will try to learn the language of their ancestry in school or in later life. In Marcus Hansen's (1952) discussion of the phenomenon of "third generation return"—grandchildren seeking to regain the lost culture of their immigrant grandparents—learning the language in school is cited as an example. Many younger respondents reported that they studied their ancestors' language as a foreign language because they wanted to get closer to their heritage or visit the country their ancestors were from. Many expressed a sense of loss that they had not been taught their ancestors' language when they were young children.

That the immigrant language is mostly lost to these later generations should not be very surprising. Yet the fragments of language maintained and the desire on the part of some people to learn the language in school show the intermittent nature of the symbolic ethnicity of people in this sample. The foreign language their immigrant ancestors once spoke survives as bits and pieces, words and phrases that are now cherished because they evoke memories of family. Language is now a voluntary part of ethnic identity—one you consciously maintain or even more actively try to recapture through courses in school.

FOOD

Food was a very important part of ethnic identity for some of the people I interviewed, particularly the Italians. No doubt some ethnically based food preferences are not consciously so, but people quite often mentioned the importance of special foods in their families. Most of these were associated with a particular holiday or event, often Christmas or Easter, not with everyday cooking.[1] This was the case for most groups except for the Italians.

The Italians I spoke with distinguished between different types of

1. It is possible that this is an artifact of the interview method. If they had been unaware of something in their diet being ethnic, they would not have mentioned it.

Italian food. Mainstream Italian food such as spaghetti and tomato sauce had no special meaning. (All my respondents, both Italian and non-Italian, reported that they frequently ate Italian food.) But there were special dishes and special ways of preparing certain types of food that were associated with Italian ethnicity. Special Italian foods reminded Christine O'Brien of enjoyable aspects of her Italian background:

> Q: Do you cook Italian food at times other than holidays?
>
> A: Yes, I don't do it all of the time, but I will make homemade pasta from scratch. I don't have the time anymore, but in fact when I was back East this time, my mother was in the hospital and I fell right into the tradition of doing the Italian side of things...I needed something to do, and Italians will find that they will cook when they have nothing else to do.

For the non-Italians in the sample, eating ethnic foods was not an everyday occurrence but an event in and of itself. Bonnie Ostrowski buys special Polish sausages whenever she goes to Chicago and when she returns she cooks them for a special family feast:

> Q: Do you still eat any Polish foods?
>
> A: Polish sausage. They sell a commercial type like at Alpha Beta or Safeway, but it isn't anything at all like what is made in the old Polish neighborhoods. Fortunately, since my husband works for the airlines, I get to fly back to Chicago two or three times a year, and I go back to the Polish neighborhood and I come back with all of these goodies. I come back with stuff from the bakery and the smoked Polish sausage and I bring it back here. And I make a traditional cookie at Christmas time and Easter time that is Polish that is called *polaski*. It has a fruit filling on top and my children and my friends all enjoy it.

Sometimes special food was eaten to celebrate an ethnic holiday. Laurie Jablonski reported that her family ate German food to celebrate Oktoberfest:

> Every fall in the town I grew up in [in Wisconsin] we would celebrate Oktoberfest, which is a German holiday. We would eat German potato salad, Polish sausage, sauerkraut, and bratwurst.
>
> Q: Do you continue to eat those kinds of foods?
>
> A: No, if I go home and someone fixes them, then I will eat them, but I never make them. In fact, I hated German potato salad.

In addition to celebrating special ethnic holidays, others celebrated American or Catholic holidays with special foods or ethnic customs to give their holidays a special "ethnic" flavor. In some households, Christmas is given an ethnic flavor by foods that are eaten only then. Many people reported that they had one or two special foods or symbolic customs that they observed at Christmas that gave the holiday an ethnic flavor. Pete Scotto: "Holidays have sort of an Italian flavor, because at the meals we have antipasto, and ravioli before we have the turkey. We drink mostly red wine." Catherine Masden described eating pirogies and kielbasa on Christmas Eve as a special Swiss custom, and Maria Reggio recounted that what made her Christmas Italian was having fish on Christmas Eve. Similarly for Susan Badovich, food was an important way in which her family showed it was Slovenian.

Often, though, the ethnic foods eaten at home when people were growing up were not seen anywhere else. So once again respondents described what they knew to be ethnic only from their own experiences in their homes. This is clear in the case of those people who only knew their own family's name for the ethnic dish they remembered from their childhood. Suzanne Benson:

Q: Did you ever eat Italian or Irish foods?

A: Spaghetti we eat all the time. Irish food, well, I don't know the name for it, the right name for it but we called it "bum's soup." It is potato soup, I guess. But I think it is different from what you would buy in a can and what most people eat.

John Davis was also a bit unsure about a dish he had grown up thinking was Czech.

My mom was proud of being Czech. She still cooks Czech meals once in a while.

Q: What kinds of things does she make?

A: There was a meal, I guess it was Czech. She calls it *fleesby*. Basically it was just a little diced ham with noodles and sauce. Then there was another thing that she called mush. Maybe it is just different names for things that everybody eats. See I am not really sure if these are Czech meals or just Czech names for other meals.

Rose Peters, too, was not quite sure, in answering this question, about what constituted Irish food. Once again the circular reasoning of attributing family traditions to ethnic traditions recurred:

Q: What kinds of Irish food did you eat?

A: Potatoes and sauerkraut. Well, I guess the sauerkraut was German.

But where my father comes from, upstate, he lived in an Irish community and that's one of the foods they ate. Lots of noodles too. There were a lot of soups. I don't know the names of them but my mother knows. I can cook a few. But we always had those foods because my father grew up with them and he liked them.

Sauerkraut is not Irish, and who knows whether the "bum's soup" that Suzanne Benson's family ate is the same as the soup Rose Peters' family consumed, or whether the Czech noodles of John Davis's family are similar to Rose Peters' Irish noodles. Of course, they may very well be different and reflective of their distinct national origins. But as each of these families has at least two different ancestries, and given the acculturation that has an Irish community in rural Pennsylvania all eating sauerkraut with their potatoes, it is natural that confusion arises in labeling particular foods as ethnic. It is clear that American families all do have cooking traditions and special family dishes that are passed along from generation to generation. But like other aspects of ethnicity examined here, the precise origins of these dishes are becoming more obscure. The construction of ethnicity through voluntary allegiance and choice allows an individual to celebrate her Irish ethnic identity by eating sauerkraut.

HOLIDAYS

When asked about the celebration of holidays, some respondents described special family customs observed on Christian holidays such as Christmas and Easter. Bonnie Ostrowski described a Polish custom that she hopes her children will keep alive:

One [thing] is not possible to do physically at Christmas. But what I do is to just talk about it in order to keep it alive. The church would make a wafer that looks very similar to what the bread is for the host now; except that it would be a square wafer and it would have a Christmas nativity scene on it. At Christmas dinner my parents would set an extra place at the table because the Christ child would be coming. And my father would take the first wafer and my mother would take the second wafer and they would hold it across each other and exchange the wafer. Then my father would break off pieces and he would say, "I wish you health, I wish you wealth, I wish you love." For each little piece that he would break off, he would eat a piece of it...Then he would do it across to each of the children, and if he and my mother knew a particular thing that that child was hoping for that Christmas, he would say, "I wish that you could get your fondest wish." Of course, there is no church here that makes this type of wafer. Even the church that I belonged to when we were growing up no longer keeps that custom alive. Of course they don't do anything like that here in California, but I like to keep it alive by just talking about traditions.

Susan Badovich observes the following Slovenian custom:

> We do the Saint Nicholas thing. We leave our shoes out for Saint Nicholas. And at Christmas I have home-baked bread and then on the table with the Christmas bread you put money, and a knife and a watch, symbolizing, there is always bread to be cut by the knife, time for heaven, or something, something about time, and that you will always have money to spend or something.

Notice that she is very interested in keeping the customs alive, but she doesn't really know what they are for. She just seems interested in maintaining some Slovenian identity. The significance of the symbols she is invoking are almost completely lost, yet Susan still tries to maintain the actions at least. In this case one can see that the "symbolic" aspect of Susan's ethnicity is quite strong, and requires some effort to maintain.

Rose Peters grew up thinking she was only Irish and Italian. As an adult she discovered from her father that he was English and Welsh in addition to being Irish. But she described only one holiday practice that she saw as especially ethnic: "My father says this comes from the Welsh. We conk eggs at Easter. You break eggs, you try to break the other person's eggs. And he says it is symbolic of the new life. So my family did that every Easter." Since Rose did not know she was part Welsh until she was an adult, she must have grown up taking part in this tradition either without knowing its origins or mistakenly believing it was Irish or Italian.[2]

One amusing story about ethnic holidays was told by the 20-year-old student Joseph Bajko. His father is Lithuanian, but they do not know any other Lithuanian people. For a while his family celebrated what Joe thought to be a special Lithuanian holiday. However, the isolation of not having anyone else to share this activity with led them to abandon it:

> We celebrated Dinakst Day. It is a holiday which is supposed to occur the Monday a week after Easter. People spray water on each other. Then when you are younger you expand it to buckets and have water wars. But we had to give it up in our house because there weren't any other Lithuanian kids

---

2. Although Rose believes that this custom is Welsh in origin, it may have originated elsewhere.

around and the kids would not understand it if you just started pouring water on them. So we stopped celebrating that holiday when we were young. We just forgot about it.

All of the Irish or part Irish respondents, and some respondents who did not have any Irish background at all, claimed to celebrate Saint Patrick's Day. This was done quite similarly in all of the households. Irish and even non-Irish people were expected to wear green, and a special dinner of corned beef and cabbage was consumed. Nobody I talked to knew why people should eat this in particular; when I asked about it, I was told that it was an "Irish" meal and that "you are supposed to eat it."[3] A few respondents reported that they had marched in the Saint Patrick's Day parade in San Francisco or other cities when they were younger. Others reported that on Saint Patrick's Day they had a party or went to a bar and a great deal of alcohol was consumed. Anne Gold reported a unique way of celebrating Saint Patrick's Day suggested by her mother's sense of humor:

Q: Were there any ethnic holidays that you celebrated?

A: Oh, yeah. Saint Patrick's Day. That is a big day. On Saint Patrick's Day my mom would wake me up first thing in the morning and she would say, "Wake up, you have to go down and get your ass painted green at City Hall."

Saint Patrick's Day was a very strong symbol of Irish identity for many of my respondents. Many of them mentioned it spontaneously in response to my questions about their ethnic identification or why they identified more with their Irish side than with other aspects of their heritage. A few Irish-American respondents expressed a great deal of disapproval about Saint Patrick's Day, however. They believed that it was an artificial symbol without meaning and that it accentuated bad stereotypes of the Irish. It had also lost much of its appeal to some Irish-identified people because of its widespread popularity and observance.

Yet even a holiday like Saint Patrick's Day, which is so widely celebrated and is so closely associated with the Irish, was often described to me in terms of family traditions and family celebrations.

3. One respondent said that he had tried to order corned beef and cabbage in Ireland, only to discover that it was difficult to get and not at all a typical meal there. Most other respondents believed that this was a typical Irish meal, and that this was why it was eaten on Saint Patrick's Day.

For example, Ellen Albert's Saint Patrick's Day party was a legend, she claimed, among her friends. She pulled out a big shamrock and showed it to me when I interviewed her. She said they put it in the front window a week before Saint Patrick's Day just to get ready. They decorated the whole house and she prepared a big meal of corned beef, cabbage, carrots, homemade bread, a green dessert of some sort, Bailey's Irish Cream, and beer. It had become a family celebration and tradition—even though Ellen Albert was only half Irish, her husband was Italian, and her children had married non-Irish people.

Those respondents who did take part in special ethnic activities on American holidays, or who observed a traditional holiday celebration that most Americans do not follow, clearly enjoyed this aspect of their ethnicity. Such activities are clearly voluntary and intermittent, but it is also clear that they bring pleasure and are relatively easy to do. People enjoy observing special holidays or observing ordinary holidays in a special way, and they like thinking that their families have distinctive traditions.

WEDDINGS AND FUNERALS

I asked each of my respondents whether weddings and funerals were in any way distinctive for members of their ethnic group and in their particular family. Irish respondents replied mostly about funerals, and Polish and Italian respondents replied mostly about weddings, with some reference to funerals too. As in other areas, individuals were unable in many cases to distinguish whether certain customs in their own families were owing to their ethnicity or simply particular to the family. In like manner it is difficult to know whether Italian-American respondents discussed weddings with me and Irish-Americans discussed funerals because of the relative weight the two different cultures attach to these events or because they are now stereotypically associated with the images of these groups. Cultural images of lavish Italian weddings, like the one in the movie *The Godfather*, and Irish wakes are ingrained in the minds of Americans. What is interesting about all of these replies is that there do not seem to be many differences in the ways in which individuals with different ancestries I talked to conduct weddings or funerals, but people thought that there were differences. Several respondents mentioned that Irish weddings involved more drinking than other types of weddings. But, for instance, Sean O'Brien was unable to tell whether this was a regional phenomenon owing to the differences between California and New York or an ethnic difference: "There might be a little more drinking at an Irish wedding than at a regular one. I have been to a lot of weddings out here and they are a little different from weddings back in New York. They are a little more partygoers back East than out here." Irish respondents were aware that the wedding is not an important Irish rite of passage in the same way that it is for other ethnic groups.

While several respondents reported that they thought Italians were supposed to have big weddings, nobody could recall anything distinctive about Italian weddings they had attended other than that the food was lavish and quite good. Elaine Williams was the only person who saw Italian weddings as particularly distinctive:

> I haven't been to one in a long time but there are lots of things that are different. The music, a lot of Italians have music usually. The cake—there is usually a cream cake instead of a regular cake. Most Italians invite kids to weddings. I don't know if they still do. Like I said, most people in my family have been married now for years, but I know any other weddings we go to there are usually no children. But at Italian weddings everybody brings their kids. The whole family comes.

Italians may perhaps be more likely to do so, but in fact many different ethnic groups have music at their weddings and allow children to attend.

Several Polish respondents stated that at Polish weddings, people would give the bridal couple money as they danced at the reception. Stan Ostrowski remembered attending weddings as a child where Polish food was served. Greg Reggio, a 48-year-old fireman, reported that at Portuguese weddings in his family, people danced special Portuguese dances. But people reported that they had not attended any weddings recently in their churches that were in any way ethnically distinctive.

Since the Irish supposedly have notorious wakes, there was a tension among my respondents about what was actually true in their experience and what they felt should be true for Irish funerals in general. Some people were very articulate about this tension, beginning their answers with, "Irish funerals are supposed to be...but my family's are..." Many people sounded almost disappointed that their family's funerals did not match up to the standards of a "true" Irish wake or funeral that they knew must exist somewhere. For instance, Pat Quinn:

They are supposed to be the traditional Irish wake but I have only been to them on the Protestant side. And, other than the fact that there are a lot of Irish people there, nothing was distinctive. The wake wasn't very lively at all actually. We just sat down and talked for a while. I mean it wasn't dismal but it wasn't merry at all and no one was passing around the Bushmills.

It may not be just because Pat's relatives were Protestant that the wakes did not live up to expectations. Ben Richter reports the same "lack of authenticity": "Well, you know the old stories about Irish wakes, where everybody had a blast, but I am not sure I have been to any. Maybe Barbara's father's, but that was just an ordinary deal, just like anybody else's."

Other respondents were much more sure that indeed there is such a thing as a particularly Irish funeral and that the funerals they have attended in their families are these Irish funerals. For instance, Patrick O'Connor:

> When my grandfather died the funeral was really boisterous. I mean here he was laying out in the casket and people were very upset but everybody was laughing. It was a celebration of his personality, which was nice because he was fun and people had fun. And I think that if there had been liquor there that people would have drunk a lot because he loved to drink. And then we had a party afterwards back at my house and people were very relaxed.

The attitude that one is not supposed to be sad at a funeral because the person is happy now that they have died was attributed specifically to the Irish by a number of respondents. However, some wondered whether this might not just be a Catholic sentiment. Dan Burke:

> They are parties. I have only been to a couple. I think a lot of it is the Catholicism too. Death is not supposed to be the end. You really are supposed to be happy for the person. Usually the sad thing about somebody dying is that you are still there and they are not and you are the one that misses them. That is my understanding of what wakes are all about.

But is having a party an Irish custom alone? Maria Reggio reports that this is what makes Italian funerals distinctive—and Chinese ones:

> I think at Italian funerals they have a party. Well, not only Italian, the Chinese do too. My father passed away when I was seventeen and I had never been to a funeral before. I was totally disgusted with it because I was very hurt. You know the family is hurt when someone passes away. You don't expect to see other people having a good time. But now I understand

it. They do have a lot of fun and it is kind of neat now that I am older. I think it is not a bad thing because you know, life goes on. Just because someone dies, it doesn't stop for the other people...I've been to so many now, and not just Italians. There are a lot of them that do that. Gathering to show the family that you care.

The custom of going back to the house for a big meal and party after the funeral was thought by many people to be Irish in origin, but no one was quite sure. Rose Peters was confused when she tried to tell me that a meal after a funeral was a particularly Italian custom and then changed her mind and wondered if it was an Irish one:

> Everybody goes to the church and then to the cemetery, and then there is a party afterwards. I have been to ones at restaurants but I think it is expected to be in the home. A lot of food. I always thought that this was not in good taste. It never made sense to me. But that is the Italian. Even though the Irish wasn't that much different now that I think about it. It was about the same. So maybe it is just upstate Pennsylvania rather than Italian or Irish.

Since Rose had only been to funerals of her relatives—and she thought some were Italian and some were Irish (although later she learned that they were also Lithuanian, Welsh, English, and French), it was natural that she might be confused as to what ethnic tradition these funeral practices came from.

Colleen Leahy Johnson (1985, 100) describes the abandonment of meals after funerals as a way in which Italians acculturate to American practices, thus implying that meals after funerals are an Italian tradition. Yet the custom seems neither a vanishing one nor particular to Italians.

Many people reported that meals after funerals were a specifically ethnic tradition in their families: they were variously described to me as an Irish, Italian, Polish, Portuguese, and Slovenian custom. I suspect, however, that they are customary among Catholics in the United States regardless of ethnic ancestry. It is understandable that funerals are particularly difficult to be sure about, since people usually only attend those of members of their families, and many respondents, especially the younger ones, had been to very few. Father Stevens, the Catholic priest in the California parish, who had conducted many funerals, said the custom of having a meal afterwards was almost universal.

Perhaps the real difference in the way different ethnic groups conduct funerals is in how people in these groups express and manage emotions. Christine O'Brien, who is both Irish and Italian, answered my question about weddings and funerals by describing these differences:

> Where do I start? I think that at the Italian wedding, even though it is a joyous occasion, there is a lot of crying. Irish weddings...Well, when Sean and I got married, his family was very reserved. My family was hugging and kissing and loving and crying. Kissy Kissy. It wasn't that his family was not loving, but they just don't demonstrate it as openly as the Italians do.
>
> Q: What about Irish and Italian funerals?
>
> A: Italian funerals, I think they hire a crier, a wailer to come to the funeral, the way that the Chinese do. Again, I haven't been to too many Italian funerals. I think on both occasions they have been sad. I think the Irish tend to make more fun of it. Not to laugh or to have disrespect. I think they tend to go over the fun times they have had with that person, where the Italians are so melancholic, and caught up in their own grief that it comes out that way.

Father Stevens said that the handling of grief and emotions was the major difference between different types of funerals he had attended:

> The Irish have notorious wakes. The Irish are not given to venting their emotion straight on. So that it is a pretty solemn thing, and there is not much emotion laid out. There are some cultural expectations. It is not culturally expected for there to be a voluble, expressive, emotional display. On the contrary, being in the job that I am in, I have seen some displays where I thought people were really hurt, and come to find out that while it was authentic and honest, once it was done, it was over. There wasn't any real lasting anything. In fact I was telling this to the funeral director yesterday when I was riding to the cemetery. I went to an Egyptian funeral once and I thought the lady was going to be in a basket when she left; she was really hysterical. That night she opened up the front door and there she was, and she said, "Father, good to see you, come on in."

To further explore the differences in the ways people handle and display emotions and the cultural expectations about behavior in family situations, let us now take a look at how people perceive those psychological differences.

CHAPTER 6

Social Psychological and Character Traits

Ethnicity may not matter too much anymore in terms of choice of marriage partner or job or place to live. It may not cause much discrimination or even everyday notice or comment. And, as we have just seen, it may not actually lead to much variation in cultural behavior. But there exists an amazingly rich, sometimes amusing, often original, and always detailed, cache of beliefs, images, stereotypes, and stories about American ethnic groups. And as Americans are increasingly of mixed background and increasingly have more latitude in how they identify themselves, the meanings consciously attached to different ethnicities and the degree of importance attached to those meanings by individuals become more significant in those choices.

In the course of my interview with Mary McGowan, I asked her to describe what certain ethnic groups are like. She told me the following story:

> I sometimes help out at lunchtime down at the church school. One of the ladies who is in charge of organizing the volunteers is a very nice woman, named Mrs. Barlow. I don't know why, but the first time she called me on the phone, I knew I liked her and I knew I would get to like her when I met her. I thought she was Irish. I really did. She has a fantastic personality and I was down there the other night and we were talking about somebody else, and she was saying this girl is real dry and doesn't have too much

personality and I said, "That's because she is not Irish." And she said, "Well, I am not Irish." And I thought, "What? Isn't that awful? Am I prejudiced or what?"

Q: What is she?

A: She is like a Heinz 57[1]—she said she had a little bit of everything. But I would have sworn she was Irish. She has a lot of personality and a good sense of humor. I thought, well, she must have some Irish in her. But she doesn't. Can you beat that?

This story is not atypical. Many of my respondents had very strong ideas about what personality characteristics, types of behavior, and traits characterize different ethnic groups. Yet the *content* of these beliefs suggests a complex combination of reality, individual family idiosyncrasies, and—for lack of a better word—creativity. For instance, did Mary McGowan's concept of Irish personality derive from an actual tendency of the Irish to be gregarious and amusing in social situations? Or from a media stereotype of the Irish as exceptionally sociable? Or from her own encounters with people whom she believed, correctly or incorrectly, to be of Irish ancestry? To what extent are the beliefs people hold about particular ethnic groups idiosyncratic and particular to specific individuals? How much is stereotype and how much truly represents "ethnic" characteristics?

As the ethnicity of later-generation middle-class Americans becomes more "symbolic" in nature, the origins of these beliefs and opinions become more obscure and their genuineness becomes more questionable, while at the same time they become more important to the very future of that ethnicity. This is because an important aspect of symbolic ethnicity is that it is voluntary and involves a degree of choice. Thus what people believe a certain ethnic identity to be is important for the identity they consciously choose to become or choose to maintain.

The character of ethnicity in my sample was such that my respondents had learned their ethnic behavior and beliefs either in the family or from the mass media. There were no intermediate groupings with fellow ethnics such as ethnic voluntary organizations or the like, and the fact that their ethnic identity was not reinforced and imposed by a wider ethnic community led to a dilemma.

---

1. "Heinz 57" was used by a number of my respondents to describe what they called a "mutt," someone who is of so many mixed ancestries that no particular one is more important than any other. The term is derived from the H.J. Heinz Company's "57 Varieties" slogan.

Because such ethnicity is increasingly created and reproduced in the absence of contact with a wider ethnic community beyond the family, it is increasingly difficult to tell what is ethnic and what is idiosyncratic to one's own family. How does one determine which of one's traits and customs are ethnic and which are family idiosyncrasies learned at an early age (with or without an ethnic label attached to them)? Many of my respondents had difficulty making those distinctions, and these difficulties led to (1) the belief that idiosyncratic or eccentric behavior that was almost surely peculiar to their own families was, in fact, shared by all members of their ethnic group, (2) the belief that values and behavior widespread throughout the American middle class were unique to their own ethnic group, or (3) reliance on stereotypes to define ethnic behavior. Examples of each of these reactions will be examined in turn.

IDIOSYNCRATIC OR ECCENTRIC BEHAVIOR

In his counseling work with people from a variety of ethnic backgrounds in situations of intermarriage that were causing strains in families, Edwin Friedman came to the conclusion that people often interpret behavior and values as ethnicity when they are actually idiosyncratic:

> What I eventually came to learn was that in any family, but particularly in easily identifiable, ethnic families, to the extent the emotional system is intense, members confuse feelings about their ethnicity with feelings about their family. The resulting inability to distinguish one from the other eventually leads to a situation in which reactions in the family relationship system are discussed with the vocabulary of the family's cultural milieu. (Friedman 1982, 506)

This confusion was evident in many of my interviews. Respondents would become uncertain as to whether traits and characteristics they were describing as "Irish" or "Polish" were ethnic or merely particular to their individual families. For instance, Patrick O'Connor answered my questions about positive or negative traits of the Irish in terms of his own family:

Q: What are the traits of Irish-Americans that you think are the best?

A: A certain amount of garrulousness. I think Irish people are less pretentious in some ways. Obviously I must be talking about myself and my family too. They are normal, basic. They don't try to intimidate you, they just try and talk. They are very up-front and they don't conceal parts of themselves, but at the same time there is something in reserve.

Q: What about the worst traits?

A: Narrow-mindedness and bigotry. In history they are famous for it. Unbelievable. And this carries on to the present day. Irish are really rednecks, I think. And then the sort of bitterness and a good memory for past sins and crimes. And also the repressiveness of sensuality in general. You know Irish cuisine sucks, and my family eats and it is over in five minutes. That is a really bad trait...a general guilt about pleasure. But at least in my family it is sort of hard to tell how much of that isn't just a Protestant[2] or a sort of American trait. They seem to dovetail pretty nicely there.

Patrick knew the stereotypes of Irish ethnicity, and he also general-ized from his experience with his family about what was ethnic and what was not. It was not that he conflated the two—he did not think that whatever his family did was Irish, or that whatever was Irish, his family did. But at times he could not really say whether what he was describing was an Irish trait or not. When I asked him if he had ever benefited from being Irish, he could not give any specific examples. But he was sure he had, because being Irish was what made his personality the way it was, and when people reacted positively to his personality, they were in fact reacting positively to his ethnicity. As he put it, "The way I am gets identified as Irish."

This confusion at times over what are family or personal traits and what are ethnic traits leads to a situation where obscure traits or customs are associated with having a particular ancestry. For in-stance, Mary McGowan:

My brother always said that the Irish favored the boys and they do. My mother even, God love her, favored the boys. I hate to admit it. I favor my boys. I don't know why. And with my own, we have five, three boys and two girls. I love my daughters dearly, but I am glad it is not the other way around. I know the Irish, they always favor their oldest son. And you really hate to admit it but it is true.

Elaine Williams described the same type of behavior in her own family as an example of one of the worst traits of Italians:

The worst trait I can think of that I associate with Italians is that, well, my dad was the head of the family and that was it. I have one brother and he

2. Patrick is not Protestant. He is referring to a Protestant American culture.

was god. The rest of us were there to sort of wait on him. I don't like that. Like the boys are really on a higher pedestal than the girls, even if there are a lot of boys. They seem to have more status in the family than the women.

People mentioned many unusual customs and characteristics that they had come to believe were owing to a particular ethnic background, which was often questionable. For instance, Cindy Betz claimed that it was Czech behavior to drink too much and not to pay any attention to your children:

Q: Are Czech people different in any way from other people?

A: As far as I can see, I went and saw my father's family and they seemed like they drink heavily. They were always drinking...their kids run around and do what they wanted. They don't really have rules...My father's niece married a black man. It's so weird because my father is so against it. He is so against it that it is not even funny. But my aunt just said, "Well, I have to accept it." That's it. I think that Czechs are just people who more or less take life as it comes. My father would not permit it. He would say, "You are not going to marry a black man. I don't care who else is, that is just it. You are not." But his family seems to be more easygoing. I never heard them yell at the kids or anything while I was there.

Of course, Cindy's logic is not the best here, because the ways in which she describes Czechs—by comparing her father's family with her father—don't make any sense. Her father is just as Czech as the rest of his family.

Joe Bajko reported that Lithuanians were known for being "warlike." He thought this explained why he was more in favor of defense spending than people of other ethnic groups. Megan O'Keefe told me that it was an Irish trait to pray out loud every time you took a trip in the car. Carol Davis argued that Irish women are well known for being very clean, good cooks, and excellent housekeepers. Finally, Joe Williams thought it was a particularly Italian custom for the mother to take care of money in the household.

Respondents thus often thought of behavior or beliefs that they had grown up with or witnessed personally as being widespread among people of the same heritage. But as people increasingly don't know the ancestry of close friends, or are of mixed ancestry themselves, or don't know any other people outside their families who are of the same ancestry, there are no independent checks on these images.

ASCRIBING VALUES TO THE GROUP

In addition to finding that people often described particular idiosyncrasies as general manifestations of ethnic behavior, I also found the opposite. People described values and beliefs that are very general—in fact, held by most middle-class Americans—as being specific to their own, and not to other, ethnic groups.

When asked about what made their ethnic group different, people almost universally ascribed certain values to it. Individuals claimed that their ethnic group was different from all the rest because of three important characteristics: (1) the high value put on the family, (2) the high value put on education, which is clear from the sacrifices of parents for their children's education, and (3) less often, but still quite common, greater loyalty to God and country. I noticed the similarities after I conducted interview after interview in which the same qualities were mentioned, but each time with a different ethnic label attached. I would be told that one family had sacrificed everything so that their children could go to college because they were Germans and Germans set great store by education. At the next house, I would be told that the Irish truly valued education, and that that was why they had finished high school when others had not. In the next house, the story would be that the Portuguese sacrificed to educate their children.

After a while I began to notice that people were all citing the same values—most often love of family, hard work, and belief in education —yet each family attributed them to their own ethnic background. As a sociologist listening to these stories, I am tempted to ascribe these values to the common American middle class of which all of my respondents were members. Yet the respondents did not learn these values as children with the label "middle-class" attached to them, but rather learned them to be "Irish," "German," or "French." The label or the symbol of the ethnic group thus links the individual and family to a wider collectivity. Such identification carries emotional and social resonance that is not available in identification with the middle class or simply with one's own family.

Ethnicity provided my respondents with a language enabling them to talk about their own extended families. In a society in which the nuclear family is the norm and the experience of most people as to what constitutes family life is limited to a very small circle—often including only members of the nuclear family—Americans have very little conceptual terminology that allows them to link their nuclear families to institutions beyond them. So when parents are trying to link their own nuclear family to the generations that went before, ethnicity is sometimes the language that is used. In this sense, the "roots" that come from knowing where your ancestors originated allow the individual family to feel a part of a wider collectivity. This was particularly noticeable in the ways in which my respondents were able to assign values and moral decisions to their ethnic groups.

The universality of this link is often missed when one focuses on just one ethnic group at a time. The universality of the emphasis on the Italian-American family is a case in point. Much of what is seen as distinctively Italian is actually common to other ethnic groups as well. A great deal has been written about Italian-Americans and the Italian-American family. Perhaps this is because the Italians were a relatively recently arrived and numerous group in the 1970s, when renewed interest in white ethnicity developed in the United States. Regardless of the reason, however, there is a lot of information available on the "Italian-American family" and the ways in which various Italians conform or do not conform to expectations about this particular family life. As Richard Alba describes it, this literature stresses the authentic ethnicity of Italian-Americans:

> Italians occupy a prominent niche in conventional imagery as representatives of what might be called "authentic" ethnicity. The standard portrait is of a group that has made the necessary cultural accommodation to American society while managing to retain its essential values, especially in the aura that suffuses the family. (Alba 1985b, 132)

Marie Rotunno and Monica McGoldrick argue that Italian-Americans value the family and its needs over those of the individual, and that this is sometimes a problem in the adjustment of individuals:

> At all times, and at all costs, family honor is to be preserved. In time of family crisis, the Italian's first recourse has been, of course, the family. The major difficulty in an Italian system develops when family and individual values conflict. (Rotunno and McGoldrick 1982, 346)

Rotunno and McGoldrick stress the importance of the Italian mother and the very large role of the extended family. They argue that the third generation does break away from the extended family, but that it manages to maintain its cultural distinctiveness. In her study of Italian-Americans in New York State, Colleen Leahy Johnson also observes that they often saw their ethnic distinctiveness in terms of close family ties (1985, 42). My respondents echoed some of these characterizations. The emphasis on the family was mentioned by almost all Italian-American respondents. Maria Reggio:

> They are very family-oriented. They like to see their family kept. They like to see the respect for the father and the mother. And in a way I feel that way too. We keep losing it as the new generations come in too. It is sad because I think it is nice to have a little respect for the older people.

Tom Scotto also described the family in the same way:

> Family is all-important for the Italian family. This is very important. Children are everything. You live your life through your children. Now sometimes that may not be the best thing. You may give them too much attention. But that is just the way that Italians are...Family, that is everything for the Italian.

His son Pete reported that he learned that family was very important for Italians from his father, very explicitly:

> Oftentimes at the dinner table he would say things like, "Oh, and always remember Italian is the best," and stuff like that. He would tell me that the family is really important. That Italian families are really strong and close. That Italians cared about each other. Whereas other ethnic groups don't have that as much, especially WASPs or people like that.

Micaela di Leonardo found this same insistence upon the role of the family among her San Francisco Bay Area Italian-American subjects. Her respondents also believed that the "Italian-American" family existed, but did not agree on any of its characteristics. Her younger respondents, like my own, often conflated ethnic and family characteristics. Her study of the ethnic kin patterns of her respondents convinced di Leonardo that the type of family structure that existed was determined by economic and material forces and was widely variable within the Italian-American community (1984, 89).

But this emphasis on family and the importance of family was not limited to Italians. Respondents from all of the different groups I interviewed all stressed reliance on family, "clannishness," and a close family as characteristic of their ethnic group. This is also true of the descriptions of different ethnic groups in a volume of advice by ethnic family therapists to other therapists on how to deal with ethnic clients (of later generations) edited by Monica McGoldrick, John K. Pearce, and Joseph Giordano under the title *Ethnicity and Family Therapy* (1982). The book is especially remarkable as a collection of opinions by these therapists about their own ethnic groups. I was struck by the ways in which each of these writers describes an emphasis on family as a trait distinctive of his or her own group. For example, Hinda Winawer-Steiner and Norbert Wetzel characterize German-Americans as showing emotional restraint, being hardworking, valuing the family highly and sacrificing to give their children a good education (ibid., 256). According to Everett Moitoza, the Portuguese in the United States are similarly characterized by the supremacy of the family unit, as well as by reliance on folk medicine practices, and a fatalistic attitude to life. The supremacy of the family means that "both children and adults are expected to gratify most of their personal, social, and emotional needs within the nuclear or extended family" and that "boundaries between extended and nuclear family membership frequently blur." (ibid., 413, 416) The Polish are likewise supposed to stress the family a great deal. Sandra M. Mondykowski emphasizes the importance of family for Polish-Americans and argues that mobility away from the extended family is looked down on (ibid, 396).

Like these authors, my respondents also in general described their respective ethnic groups' reliance on family as a positive trait. However, there were a few respondents for whom this emphasis on family became oppressive. Lisa Paulo:

> Family, that is the biggie. You have to do this because it is family. Give me a break. I am tired of doing this because of family. What if I do not want to see the family? But you are not supposed to say that...There are people in my extended family who I just don't like. They are mean and backbiting and I just don't like spending time with them. But I have to.

Christine O'Brien reported that the closeness of the family was a wonderful thing when you needed its support, but that it could be stifling when you were trying to assert your own individuality. She said that the closeness in her family was enforced by a sense of guilt about being in any way independent of it. When she moved away from New York with her husband, it caused a giant family crisis:

> Guilt, doing things because the traditions of the family. That is the way that they did it. You had better do it that way too. Breaking away, marrying someone and moving away, that was taking the piece of the apple out of the apple. Because everybody tended to stay close to the core of the family...But I remember my mother tried to break the marriage up, to keep me close to her. "Don't leave me. How could you leave me?" And the tears! That is what is so hard to get over and I don't want to instill that in my kids. I think that the Italians have done that.

Pete Scotto also complained that this emphasis on closeness in the Italian family was interfering with his ability to live his life as he pleased: "I think that Italian kids are expected to be more family-oriented than their non-Italian friends. I think that in a way they have less freedom to sort of go and do stuff."

This emphasis on family, which is a legacy in part of an immigrant culture, and a positively ranked value in American middle-class culture, was perceived by respondents as being something quite specific to their own cultural backgrounds. Researchers who concentrate or study one ethnic group at a time do not see how widespread and common such values are.

STEREOTYPES

Of course, many of the ideas people have about other ethnic groups come from the stereotypes that exist in popular thought. And in fact people also derive some ideas about their own ethnic groups from stereotypes. People also measure their own experiences and beliefs against prevailing stereotypes—accepting or rejecting the images they are presented with based on their own knowledge.

Sometimes people will derive images even of their own ethnic group from a combination of media images and personal experience. For instance, Mary McGowan answered my questions by referring to books that she had read, or to her son's "professional" Irishness:

Q: What are the worst traits of the Irish?

A: A big problem with the Irish is the drinking. I didn't realize this until many years ago, I read a story, I can't remember the name of the poet, but he was a great actor and a poet and he drank a lot. He was an alcoholic. I read his life story. He was born in Ireland and the reason he drank so much, he was born in Ireland during the famine and it was a feat to get food, but if you could drink, you were like rich, and that is how he became an alcoholic...Stubbornness too...My son has a T-shirt that says, "You can always tell an Irishman, but you can't tell him much." He is the one of my kids who is very up on the Irish. He has all of this Irish stuff, and he has done the family tree and all. It is nice I guess. I don't have time for it myself. He can do it and tell me.

Laurie Jablonski, who is of German and Polish descent, answered all my questions about Polish characteristics in terms of stereotypes of the Poles, but replied differently when I asked about the Germans. She mentioned some of her relatives:

> I guess I think of German people, German-American people, as like my mom's side of the family. I think of my grandmother and how she described her family or her parents and stuff as being serious and hard-working. Not getting a whole lot of joy out of life. That life was a struggle, which may be related to the times that they lived in, but I sort of think of it as being German in some sense too.

When I asked about the stereotypes people had of the Germans, those same ideas were mentioned again:

> The German stereotype is sort of hardworking and serious and sort of a Protestant culture. I have been to Germany and people seemed kind of serious and hardworking. I think a lot of the stereotypes of German people come from World War II. Hitler and Nazis. People think of Germans that way, as sort of cold people.

The interaction of stereotypes with personal experience is evident here, as Laurie was aware of stereotypes of Germans and of the ways in which her mother's side of the family fit at least some of them.

The family of Joyce Hoffman, who is of German, Scottish, and English descent, had no contact with other German-Americans and did not even think of themselves as German-American until her mother decided that that was what they were. Thus they got their idea of what it meant to be German from stereotypes and family eccentricities:

> Q: What kind of information did your parents give you about what it means to be German?
>
> A: Well, that's just it. It was all my mother and she didn't really know. So it was the food. Fattening food and beer. We didn't know any other German people and my mother wasn't German so I don't really know how she even knew how Germans were supposed to be. We were growing up on military bases and the only people that we knew were Japanese war brides and for some reason we knew some Hungarians.

However, this did not stop Joyce from having her own ideas of what German-Americans were like. She mentioned being "hardworking" as the Germans' best trait, and being very dour and sober as their worst trait. She had also developed ideas about how German families were different from other families:

> I have my stereotypes on how German family values are different for Germans. But it is not based on my family. I mean maybe I get this

information from my family, but I get the feeling that Germans are very serious and have sober kinds of families. Other kinds of families have fun together somehow, but Germans aren't like that. They are very work-oriented or something. You know they are not so oriented toward having holidays together and things like that.

Q: Well, is that what your family is like?

A: Well, sort of, yeah. I don't know. Somehow the stereotype of the Germans seems separate from my family. The German stereotype is sort of [a] purer strain of what my family was.

The characteristics these individuals mentioned as being specific to their particular groups were thus derived either from books and the mass media or from firsthand knowledge of their own particular families. But in both cases there is uncertainty attached to these characteristics—either your own family's behavior and personalities don't match the expectations derived from the stereotypes, or the behavior and characteristics of your family stand alone. Because these individuals do not have much day-to-day contact with other families and individuals who share their ethnicity—as one would if one lived in an ethnically segregated neighborhood—the behavior and characteristics they associate with the group come either from close family members or from impersonal media accounts.

In an article on stereotypes and their social origins and implications, Stanley Lieberson (1982) predicts that members of stereotyped ethnic groups will generally accurately perceive or recount the stereotypes others have of their ethnic group. They also know the jokes other groups may make about them. I found this to be true among the people I interviewed. I asked people if they knew what American stereotypes of the Irish were and whether or not they were valid. Sean O'Brien:

A: A bunch of drunks and fighters and hell-raisers.

Q: Is there any validity to it?

A: Yes. I was one myself. I haven't had a drink in twenty-six years, but I used to have a fifth of whiskey a day, with beer on top of that. I was known to have a drink on a hot summer's day and every day was a hot summer's day. I think the Irish have a reputation to have a good laugh, a good time, raise hell.

Barbara Richter:

Q: What is the stereotype of the Irish?

A: Boisterous, full of baloney, good for a story any time. Good drinker.

Q: Where do you think they get this idea?

A: From the people themselves. I think Irish people are very colorful. They would go on and on about nothing. I think that is a true picture of them. They are fantastic storytellers. They are very colorful. I don't think they are dull people, and they like to have a good time. But there is a very sad side too. It is hard to believe that people can be so narrow, since we all live in this modern world.

Mary McGowan knew that people reacted to her based on common stereotypes:

Q: So when you meet people, they don't comment on the fact that you are Irish?

A: Every once in a while they will say that they can tell that you are Irish because you have a great sense of humor. Some garbage like that. Especially when you have had a few drinks. Then they want you to sing a few songs.

This is an interesting contradiction. Mary McGowan recognizes this as a stereotype that is not necessarily true, but recall from the beginning of this chapter that she made the same assumptions when she met her new friend with a sense of humor at the parish school. She just assumed that her new friend was Irish because she had a sense of humor.

Even if they did not necessarily think others could identify them as members of a particular group, they did not wish to contribute to unfavorable stereotypes. Bill Kerrigan expressed disdain for people who "parade" their Irishness, conforming to stereotypes of what it means to be Irish. He described an uncle of his who was "into being Irish": "My mom's brother really feels that he's Irish. He plays the bagpipes. And we all just want to turn around. I mean this is sick. You are not really that Irish and its fine to be proud that you are Irish but to go a little overboard..." He believed his father's Irishness was much more authentic, but notice that it is also much more family-based, tied directly to experience of his immigrant grandfather:

My father will manifest his Irishness by talking a lot about Grams. He will mention Irish history every once in a while. I don't really know how he does it. I know when he was younger he used to make cakes in the kitchen with guns in them and send them to Ireland. But he has not done that in a while.

Bill McGowan, a 62-year-old retired army officer, expressed disdain

for Irish-Americans who blindly support the IRA without any knowledge of the situation in Northern Ireland:

> Q: What do you think about the American Irish who are into supporting
>   the IRA?
>
> A: I think basically they do not know a whole lot about it. I think maybe
>   they are caught up in their Irish identity and that is something to hold
>   on to, something to support it. Even though they don't know how
>   much destruction goes on.

Pete Scotto described negative traits of Italians as being the loud-
ness and brutality of Italian men, and pride in being ignorant. He
reported feeling bad when he was traveling in Italy because the men
were behaving in such a macho manner. He felt somehow responsible
or guilty that Italian men behaved in what he considered to be such a
negative fashion.

I asked all respondents, Italians and non-Italians, about the characteristics and traits of Italian-Americans. The answers of both
groups provide some information about the ways in which in-group
and out-group members define the groups. One thing was clear—both
the Italians and the non-Italians were aware of negative stereotypes of
the group.

My Italian-American respondents had a partially distorted view of
what non-Italians thought of them. The Italian-Americans I interviewed mostly claimed that non-Italians had negative stereotypes or
images of them. Janet Albert Parro thinks that non-Italians think that
Italians are "big, fat, dirty wine drinkers." Most Italian-Americans
thought that non-Italians thought of the Mafia as the stereotype of
Italians. While these expectations were borne out by the reactions of
the non-Italians in my sample, it was actually a much more varied
picture that they reported than just the single gangster image. Like the
Italian-American respondents, the non-Italians mentioned the warm,
happy extended family, which they viewed as a source of support for
individuals. No one mentioned a drawback to this strong family. They
also mentioned Italian food quite often, stressing how important food
is to authentic Italian ancestry.

In fact, "Italian" was the most common response by people to the
question, "If you could be a member of any ethnic group you wanted,
which one would you choose?" The main reasons given were the
belief that Italians had a warm family life and that they had excellent
food. Italian was also most often chosen for the ancestry of children

in mixed marriages when parents simplified a child's ancestry on the census form. It is, in other words, a very popular choice of ancestry.

The main difference between the characterizations of Italian ethnicity by the non-Italians as opposed to the Italian-Americans is that the non-Italians included a lot more negative elements. Every single non-Italian mentioned the Mafia and gangsters in depicting Italian-Americans. Most of them said they must have gotten that idea from the media, although one woman reported that her brother-in-law had been an altar boy at Mafia funerals and that that was where she had made the association between Italians and organized crime.

The other negative images mentioned were being dirty; being loud; fighting a lot, not talking; being afraid of people; having a penchant for enjoying life rather than working; being selfish; having fat women, domineering husbands, and submissive wives; having husbands who cheated on their wives; being temperamental, weak individuals with an excessive reliance on the family; and being unambitious and not very bright. At the same time, Italians were characterized as being from warm supportive families; having beautiful women; being able and willing to show love and affection to one another; having excellent food; being exceptionally clean housekeepers; valuing education highly; doing well in business; getting along well with Jews and Greeks; dressing well; and being fun at parties.

An equal number of people reported that Italians were exceptionally clean and that they were exceptionally dirty. Rose Peters, whose mother was Italian and whose father was Irish, reported that the Italian woman took pride in her home and cleaned it thoroughly and often. Her mother had told her, though, that the Irish were very dirty and had too many kids to keep a clean home.

On the other hand, Cindy Betz described an unflattering portrait of Italians, and what she believed to be the origin of this image:

> Oh, everyone thinks that Italians are little Guidos with black hair. They are stupid and they are greaseballs.
>
> Q: Where do you think that image comes from?
>
> A: Well, when they first came over here. In fact, I know for a fact—my mother has told me that in Italy they don't take a bath every day. They don't shave. It's disgusting, but it's true. A lot of Europeans don't. They came over here and they probably only took a bath once a week and that is why they called them greaseballs. Their hair was greasy, and I guess people thought that if you do any kind of manual labor

then you are not that bright. I guess putting bricks up against the wall doesn't take that much intelligence.

This knowledge of negative stereotypes was true of non-Italians as well: both Bonnie Ostrowski and Laurie Jablonski knew about the ways in which Americans thought of Poles. Bonnie Ostrowski:

I think they make us out to be slow and bumbling...Americans just mix us together with those other people, Russians and the Slovaks and so forth. They don't have that opinion of the French and English but they do of all the Middle European people. It is not true, but I think Americans do.

When asked whether these Polish jokes and stereotypes bothered her, Bonnie replied that they did not:

If they want to make us out to be slow or stupid or bumbling that doesn't bother me. Unless they are in extremely poor taste...I think that is one of the redeeming features about Polish people. They like to laugh. They like to joke, and I think that they themselves like to make jokes about Polish people. In fact, I think a Polish joke sounds funnier when a Polish person tells it.

Laurie Jablonski was also aware of the negative stereotypes of Polish-Americans, and it was, in fact, the only image she reported having of what it meant to be Polish-American:

Well, there is a stereotype. The stereotype of being really stupid...They are also supposed to be incompetent. It is not a very glamorous or cool thing to be. It's not like being Swedish or anything. To be Swedish is to be sexy...I have never been to Poland so I don't really know. It's not a country that is very wealthy or has a lot of glamour associated with it.

But Laurie was not bothered by these stereotypes or Polish jokes:

Q: Do jokes about Polish people bother you?

A: Not really. I sort of feel like they should. But they really don't. Because my father would always tell them. It would just be this funny thing...I never really thought that people were saying that Polish people were stupid...It was just something that was just this custom to tell Polish jokes. My dad seemed to have a lot of fun being Polish. Seems to still. It's like a joke kind of thing. He would make jokes and he would get some attention for being Polish.

LACK OF AN ETHNIC IMAGE

Identification with a particular ethnic group, even when it is quite vocal, does not necessarily mean that the individual has a strong idea of what that ethnicity entails. One can have a strong sense of identity without a specific idea of that identity meaning anything. And one's conception of the ethnic group does not necessarily come from personal experience anymore—thus some people had more of a fixed opinion of Italians than of their own ethnicity.

A few of my respondents who were quite adamant in their Irish self-identification stated that it was quite important to them that their ancestors had come from Ireland. But they could not describe any ways in which the Irish were different from other Americans. For instance, Bill McGowan:

> I think family values are pretty much the same for everyone. I think pretty much all groups are equal. I just think people have some sorts of stereo-types about different things. Like you could say, "Oh, Irish, big, happy loving family." But you could say that about anybody else too.

Pat Quinn was incredulous that I would even ask the question:

> Q: Do you think there is such a thing as an Irish-American character?
>
> A: I don't know. Not that I have ever noticed. Maybe there is and it is so ingrained that I don't even notice it.
>
> Q: What are the traits of Irish-Americans that you think are the best?
>
> A: I have no idea. Do other people really have answers to this question?

Sean O'Brien, who comes across as a "professional Irishman," also surprised me with his answer to this question:

> A: Traits of Irish-Americans? I think there are no real traits. Irish-Americans are the same as anyone else when it comes to traits because of the generations. Like my kids are three or four generations removed and they are just like anybody else...I don't see that you'll see the traits now in myself because we are too far removed. We are into the American way of living and not the old Irish way.
>
> Q: It is interesting that you say you would give an Irish person a second look and you have this affinity for other Irish people and then you don't really think there is anything different about Irish people.
>
> A: It is just the bloodline or something. They are ancestors come from the old country. That is enough.

Most people who did not have a specific notion of what Irish-Americans are like answered my question by describing Irish people in Ireland rather than Irish-Americans. Perhaps this is because Irish-Americans have been in the country for so long that many are very assimilated, and because Americans have a great deal of knowledge about people in Ireland.

Greg Reggio does not believe that there are differences between Portuguese-Americans and other Americans:

> I think that the Portuguese, sort of like the Irish, have managed to sort of melt into what the American is. They have sort of more truly accepted the melting-pot theory and melted in. When I think of a Portuguese-American, I can think of an Irish-American and other nationalities and they would sort of all go together now.

In fact, for some people this lack of an ethnic image is precisely what is attractive about a particular ethnicity. Catherine Masden liked being Swiss precisely because she did not really know what it meant:

> It is the least stereotypical ethnic group. I don't know what the ideal image of a Swiss person is, but nobody else does either because it is a small country. Because the Swiss aren't really talked about. I mean it is not like Poland or the Polish. We are not made fun of in any way. Because we are the least in numbers. It's not like if I was Irish and we could say, "Oh, they drink, they have tempers." A lot of people I know live up to those expectations, which is probably how they got the name. Swiss are so uncommon.

And Ted Jackson said that he would choose to be French in an ideal situation, because the French "don't have an image like all the other ethnics do. They don't have to fit into some stereotype. They can be themselves."

These individuals all said in other parts of their interviews that having an ethnic identity was very important to them. They all actively tried to maintain it in some form or other—yet they also either claimed that they were no different from other ethnic groups, like Sean O'Brien, or valued their own ethnicity precisely because it did not have any particular content, either for them or for others, like Catherine Masden or Ted Jackson. These rather extreme cases reinforce a central point about symbolic ethnicity. There is something rewarding merely in having an ethnic identity—completely apart from the content or implications of that ethnicity. In the next chapter we explore this apparent paradox.

CHAPTER 7

The Costs of
a Costless Community

What does claiming an ethnic label mean for a white middle-class American? Census data and my interviews suggest that ethnicity is increasingly a personal choice of whether to be ethnic at all, and, for an increasing majority of people, of which ethnicity to be. An ethnic identity is something that does not affect much in everyday life. It does not, for the most part, limit choice of marriage partner (except in almost all cases to exclude non-whites). It does not determine where you will live, who your friends will be, what job you will have, or whether you will be subject to discrimination. It matters only in voluntary ways—in celebrating holidays with a special twist, cooking a special ethnic meal (or at least calling a meal by a special ethnic name), remembering a special phrase or two in a foreign language. However, in spite of all the ways in which it does not matter, people cling tenaciously to their ethnic identities: they value having an ethnicity and make sure their children know "where they come from."

In this chapter I suggest two reasons for the curious paradox posed by symbolic ethnicity. First, I believe it stems from two contradictory desires in the American character: a quest for community on the one hand and a desire for individuality on the other. Second, symbolic ethnicity persists because of its ideological "fit" with racist beliefs.

AMERICAN VALUES AND SYMBOLIC ETHNICITY

Analysts of American culture have long noticed the fundamental tension between the high values Americans place on both individuality and conformity. Writing over a hundred years ago on the American psyche and character, Alexis de Tocqueville developed a theme that has been a recurrent observation of all students of the nature of American character—the tension between the conflicting values of individualism and conformity, or between self-reliance and cooperation. In fact, Tocqueville coined the term *individualism* to describe the particular way in which people in America "turned in on themselves" all of their feelings and beliefs:

> Individualism is a calm and considered feeling which disposes each citizen to isolate himself from the mass of his fellows and withdraw into the circle of family and friends; with this little society formed to his task, he gladly leaves the greater society to look after itself. (Tocqueville [1835–39] 1969, 506)

Tocqueville noticed that while individualism led people to find their own beliefs within themselves, this isolation was at the same time compatible with conformity, because people are constantly looking for affirmation of those beliefs in the people around them. Contrasting democratic societies with aristocratic ones, Tocqueville argues that while "knowing your place" in an aristocratic society binds individuals to their ancestors and descendants, the peculiar effect of democracy is to isolate individuals from one another and from the generations that precede and follow them:

> As social equality spreads there are more and more people who, though neither rich or powerful enough to have much hold over others, have gained or kept enough wealth and enough understanding to look after their own needs. Such folk owe no man anything and hardly expect anything from anybody. They form the habit of thinking of themselves in isolation and imagine that their whole destiny is in their own hands.
>
> Thus not only does democracy make men forget their ancestors, but also clouds their view of their descendants and isolates them from their contemporaries. Each man is forever thrown back on himself alone, and there is danger that he may be shut up in the solitude of his own heart. (Tocqueville [1835–39] 1969, 508)

Tocqueville saw the uniquely American proclivity for joining voluntary groups—associations of all different kinds—as a necessary moderating influence on this individualism. By participation in these small groups—local government and communities—Americans would find the sense of connection to others that would inoculate them from the dangers of despotism. Without these communities, the danger of a mass society of isolated individuals is that they are easy prey to despots taking advantage of a democratic system.

Since Tocqueville first noticed this tension between individualism and conformity, it has been a central theme in discussions of the nature of American culture and character. Rupert Wilkinson, in *The Pursuit of American Character* (1988), a review of writing on American character between 1940 and 1980, argues that the dual attraction of Americans to individualism and community is the overriding theme of all accounts of American character in this period. He argues that the course from the 1940s to the 1980s was full circle, starting with a renewed interest in Tocqueville's concern with individualism, proceeding through a period of concern with social pressure and conformity in books like David Riesman's *The Lonely Crowd* and William H. Whyte's *The Organization Man*, and then returning to a concern with unstable, isolating egoism in Christopher Lasch's *The Culture of Narcissism* and Robert Bellah et al.'s *Habits of the Heart*.

Describing the situation in the 1980s and the most recent books examining the elusive "American character," Wilkinson focuses on the concern of these authors with the conflict "between modern American culture and deep yearnings for community," and a renewed stress on the problems caused for people by social atomism, rather than conformity.[1]

Wilkinson asks the interesting question of whether this shift reflects merely a change in writers' sensibilities or an actual change in American behavior and values. He suggests that the massive suburbanization that has occurred since the 1940s may have led to this move on the part of most Americans away from extensive involvement in community:

> Suburbia itself may have become less communal...[one] sees a mass of over-equipped houses and yards which have become small, private islands. Front porch society, where everyone met everyone, has been closed down by domestic technology: the automobile, electronic entertainment, and air conditioning. Families either vanish indoors (or into their backyards) or whisk themselves away on wheels. (Wilkinson 1988, 43)

1. Wilkinson cites recent works such as Bellah et al.'s *Habits of the Heart*, Yankelovich's *New Rules: Searching for Self-Fulfillment in a World Turned Upside Down*, and Slater's *The Pursuit of Loneliness: American Culture at the Breaking Point*.

The people I have been describing in this book are the families that live in these suburbs and live these lives, and it is possible that the isolation described here is in part responsible for the expressed wishes of some of my respondents for more "community." Symbolic ethnicity fulfills this particularly American need to be "from somewhere." Having an ethnic identity is something that makes you both special and simultaneously part of a community. It is something that comes to you involuntarily through heredity, and at the same time it is a personal choice. And it allows you to express your individuality in a way that does not make you stand out as in any way different from all kinds of other people. In short, symbolic ethnic identity is the answer to a dilemma that has deep roots in American culture.

THE ELEMENT OF CHOICE

Symbolic ethnicity was appealing to my respondents for another reason as well—the element of choice involved. In a contemporary study of the strategies of successful advertising campaigns devised by Madison Avenue firms, William O. Beeman describes how clever advertisers devise ad campaigns that appeal simultaneously to the opposite values of individuality and conformity. He adds another important theme, freedom of choice. Freedom of choice, writes Beeman, quoting the advertisers, "comes close to being sacred for Americans." People must be persuaded that they are meeting contradictory goals in selecting the advertiser's product: making a choice that shows their individuality while at the same time giving them membership in a group—the group of people who have made the same choice. He writes:

> In the United States, through exercise of individual choice, people not only demonstrate their uniqueness, they also recognize and actualize their integration with others. They do this by making, acknowledging, and perpetuating social ties based solely on the affinity that arises through making the same choices. (Beeman 1986, 59)

Of course, it is the job of the advertiser to convince people that purchasing a product makes them part of a group. The group of people one feels a part of may not exist in any real sense as a group, existing only within the framework of the advertisement itself: "By buying a Pepsi you take place in an exchange, not only of money, but of yourself as a Pepsi person. You have become special, yet one of a clan: however, you do not meet those others, except *in* the advertisement" (Williamson 1978, 53).

Beeman claims that advertisers who create successful campaigns based on combining these American values have a very persuasive and attractive package prepared for the target audience. In fact, he describes it as a surefire recipe for success:

> These double messages are remarkable in that they tell consumers they can achieve contradictory but laudable goals merely by exercising choice on a microcosmic level. Every time we choose one brand of liquid detergent or motor oil over another, we are subtly being told both: "you are unique and special" and "you are in the company of the millions of others who choose this." This is the opposite of a no-win situation. It is an always-win situation in cognitive terms, and it is as powerful as it is subtle. (Beeman 1986, 64)

I have been describing symbolic ethnicity throughout this book as embodying a great deal of choice. Even among those who have a homogeneous background and do not need to choose an ancestry to identify with, it is clear that people do choose to keep an ethnic identity. And until recently many social scientists who have attempted to understand this persistence of ethnic identity have looked at the nature of the particular ethnic groups—extolling the virtue of particular strands of the ethnic culture worth preserving. Yet if one looks at ethnicity almost as though it were a product one would purchase in the marketplace—Stein and Hill's "dime store" ethnics—one can see that symbolic ethnic identity is an attractive product.

The choice to have a symbolic ethnicity—in all the ways I have described—is an attractive and widespread one despite its lack of demonstrable content, because having a symbolic ethnicity combines individuality with feelings both of community and of conformity through an exercise of personal choice. These themes recur throughout my interviews.

Part of the reason that ethnicity is so appealing to people is evident in the reasons people give to the question of *why* they "like being ethnic." Being ethnic makes them feel unique and special and not just "vanilla," as one respondent put it. They are not like everyone else. At the same time, being ethnic gives them a sense of belonging to a collectivity. It is the best of all worlds: they can claim to be unique and special while simultaneously finding the community and conformity with others that they also crave. But that "community" is of a type that will not interfere with a person's individuality. The closest this type of ethnic identity brings a person to "group activity" is something like a Saint Patrick's Day parade. It is not as if these people belong to ethnic voluntary organizations or gather as a group in churches or neighborhood or union halls. They work and reside within the mainstream of American middle-class life, yet they retain the interesting benefits—the "specialness" of ethnic allegiance.

An exaggerated way of examining the reasons behind these choices is through a question I asked that freed respondents from any constraint based on the belief that ethnicity is inherited. I asked people, "If you could be a member of any ethnic group you wanted, which one would you choose?" It is clear from the answers that having an ethnic identity gives people a feeling of "specialness" and fulfills a longing for community. Liz Field articulates this "hunger for ethnicity":

> I would like to be a member of a group that is living a culture, like on an American Indian reservation, or a gypsy encampment...or an Italian neighborhood. Where there is some meat to the culture. Mine was very wishy-washy. There was not much to make it strong and appealing. It was just supposed to be this thin little rod in the back of my spine. Scotch Irish. It was thin. It was diluted. I would like to be in a rich cultural society. I don't know which one it would be. Whichever one is the richest...Where they have a tight familial structure of aunts and uncles and cousins. And they all know their second cousins intimately and they are all involved in each other's lives. Which didn't happen to me. Although cousins lived nearby, we weren't tight. We didn't know if they were in town. We were just not as aware of them as I think other ethnic groups are, the ones that are rich and the ones that are tight. It could be Alaskan Eskimo. I mean, I am on my own here. I don't have that many friends. I do my work. I play my instrument. I travel a lot. But I don't have a big cultural...People who have stayed where they grew up have a larger cultural...Well, I don't even have it at home, where my mother lives. It has just not been there for me, ever. The kind of thing where you know everybody and you know all the back roads. There is a richness there. Maybe that is what draws me to some rich, thick, culture. [Laughs.] But flexible too, open to new ideas. [Laughs again.]

What Liz Field ironically adds at the end of her description of the "thick culture" she craves shows that even those who hunger for a romanticized version of an all-encompassing ethnic community realize that they only want the positive aspects of that community. Liz wants the warmth of a close community without the restrictions that she admits usually accompany such a community. But while Liz fantasizes that the warmth and familial ties missing from her own life would be present if she were American Indian or a gypsy, in fact, the situation she describes is precisely what a symbolic ethnic identity gives to middle-class Americans—a sense of rich culture through a community with no cost to the other contradictory values we also crave: individuality, flexibility, and openness to new ideas.

In fact the very idea that Americans have of "community" is very much tied up in their minds with ethnicity. Ethnicity is sometimes defined as family writ large. The image that people conjure up of "community" is in part one based on common origins and interests. The concrete nature of those images in America is likely to be something like a small town or an ethnic ghetto, while in many other parts of the world this sense of peoplehood or community might be realized through nationalist feelings. As noted in chapter 3, the idea of being "American" does not give people a sense of one large family, the way that being French does for people in France. In America, rather than conjuring up an image of nationhood to meet this desire, ethnic images are called forth.

The immensely popular book *Habits of the Heart* exemplifies the invocation of ethnicity as an example of community. The authors diagnose the problems with Americans as stemming from a lack of community—a community that people really want, but lack even a language to talk about, because it challenges the independence they have traditionally valued. Bellah et al. mourn the passing of the strong ethnic ties that vanish as Americans move into the middle class. They cite in contrast "ethnic and racial communities, each with its own story and its own heroes and heroines" as examples of "genuine communities" of memory (p. 153). The optimal solution for Bellah et al. would be if people belonged to a community of memory—a community people do not "choose," but are born into, where people inherit a commitment to traditional ties.[2]

The "thick culture" and tradition that Liz Field described is in Americans' minds associated with strong ethnic groups. But Liz has recognized the crucial point that precisely what we crave about

---

2. If Americans cannot have that type of community, the authors of *Habits of the Heart* suggest, the next best thing for people to do is to go back to church. Wilkinson notes that Bellah et al. do not tell their readers that "such communities can be oppressive, snoopy, and stultifying. Conversely, they underestimate the satisfactions of being able to create and select one's social networks, and the sheer vitality of association that comes from working at it out of a fear of being isolated" (Wilkinson 1984, 44). Wilkinson's direct answer to such solutions is, I think, absolutely correct and is also echoed in the remarks just quoted from Liz Field.

community and tradition is also tied to things we don't crave—conformity, lack of change, and rigidity. The maintenance of boundaries around a community involves costs to the individuals inside as well as providing the benefits of nurturance and security. Community seen one way is warm and nurturing; seen another, it is stifling and constricting.

This is the essential contradiction in American culture between individuality and community. Thus Liz Field's ironic comment that she wanted a thick culture that was also flexible and open to new ideas indicates the fact that she is very American. She wants both. And I think this is the best way to understand the symbolic ethnicity I have described—it gives middle-class Americans at least the appearance of both: conformity with individuality; community with social change. And as an added bonus—which almost ensures its appeal to Americans—the element of choice is also there. Ethnicity has a built-in sense of appeal for Americans that should make Coke and Pepsi envious. Madison Avenue could not have conspired to make a better and more appealing product. This partly explains the patterns in the choices people make about their ethnic identities. When given a choice, whites will choose the most "ethnic" of the ancestries in their backgrounds.

Over and over again people told me that they liked keeping an ethnic identity because it gave them a sense of who they were, where they had come from, and, as one respondent said, made them "more interesting." And the more unusual your ancestry sounds, the more "interesting" you are. Cindy Betz:

> I work in an office and a lot of people in there always talk about their background. It's weird because it is a big office and people are of all different backgrounds. People are this or that. It is interesting I think to find out. Especially when it is something that you don't hear a lot about. Something that is not common like Lithuania or something. That's the good part about being Czech. People think it is something different.

Joe Bajko felt that being Lithuanian made him feel special:

> It's nice to feel that you are one of a thousand. You are not exactly in a big crowd. In fact, rarely do you find any Lithuanians around. It's nice to feel that you are in an elite group. Like in grade school, when everyone would brag, like saying, "I'm Italian," I would say, "I'm Lithuanian."

Those who don't have a strong ethnic identity or who don't have an ancestry in their past that makes them feel special or interesting feel as though they should at least hold on to what they do have. Ted Jackson:

> It gives you something to identify with. Lets you know where you are coming from. Something to hold on to. It is something that no one can take away from you. Something that is all yours...When everyone else has something. And if you are not Italian, or whatever, and you don't have these strong ethnic identities or just things that come with it—all these celebrations and activities and all that...if you don't have that and everyone else is going here and going there...it makes you feel kind of left out. Yeah, I really do think you have to have something.

Again and again the same message comes through. You have to have something you can identify with. If it is a "special" ethnicity, you can be interesting or elite, but nevertheless you must have something. And if, like Ted Jackson, the identity you have to hold on to is being part Irish, French, Scottish, German, and English, you celebrate and hold on to that identity. In Ted's case he says he feels closest to the French part, but it is the maintenance of an identity, any identity, that people strive for. Again Liz Field describes why her ethnicity, even though it is not of a rich culture, is so important to her:

> While I don't feel that my ethnic heritage needs to be dominant in my awareness, I do have an awareness of it and I am encouraged to learn a bit more about the type of people I may have come from. The type of traditions that I might have way back there somehow gotten exposed to. By knowing OK, I am X and X, or XY and Z. Then I don't have to pay any more attention to it. If you know what I mean. It's like OK, there, that is solved now. And you move on. It's important to be something. I need an awful lot of help in defining myself and that is a tool. A piece of information that puts a boundary on things.

Symbolic ethnicity is thus not something that will easily or quickly disappear, while at the same time it does not need very much to sustain it. The choice itself—a community without cost and a specialness that comes to you just by virtue of being born—is a potent combination.

SYMBOLIC ETHNICITY AND RACE

But what of the consequences of this symbolic ethnicity? Is it a harmless way for Saturday suburban ethnics to feel connected and special? Is it a useful way to unite Americans by reminding us that we

are all descended from immigrants who had a hard time and sacrificed a bit? Is it a lovely way to show that all cultures can coexist and
that the pluralist values of diversity and tolerance are alive and well in
the United States?

The answer is yes and maybe no. Because aside from all of the
positive, amusing, and creative aspects to this celebration of roots and
ethnicity, there is a subtle way in which this ethnicity has consequences for American race relations. After all, in much of this discussion the implicit and sometimes explicit comparison for this symbolic
ethnicity has been the social reality of racial and ethnic identities of
America's minority groups. For the ways in which ethnicity is flexible
and symbolic and voluntary for white middle-class Americans are the
very ways in which it is not so for non-white and Hispanic Americans.

Thus the discussions of the influence of looks and surname on
ethnic choice would look very different if one were describing a
person who was one-quarter Italian and three-quarters African-
American or a woman whose married name changed from O'Connell
to Martinez. The social and political consequences of being Asian or
Hispanic or black are not symbolic for the most part, or voluntary.
They are real and often hurtful.

So for all of the ways in which I have shown that ethnicity does not
matter for white Americans, I could show how it does still matter very
much for non-whites. Who your ancestors are does affect your choice
of spouse, where you live, what job you have, who your friends are,
and what your chances are for success in American society, if those
ancestors happen not to have been from Europe. Whether this is a
temporary situation, and the experience of non-whites in America
will follow the same progression as the experience of these white
ethnic groups, has been one of the central questions in American
social science writing on this subject. The question, then, of whether
ethnic groups such as Italians and Poles are in some way the same as
minority groups such as Chicanos and blacks is a complicated one—
both analytically and politically. Analytically, social scientists have
tried to assess the assimilation process of white ethnics and non-white
groups to ascertain whether the American opportunity structure will
open up for non-whites. Politically, this issue is also an important
one—especially with the development of affirmative action legislation
and the Voting Rights Act, which moved to provide legal protection
and special attention to what were defined as "minority groups"

subject to discrimination, as opposed to ethnic groups who were not. Stephen Steinberg (1981) and others writing on the ethnic revival of the 1970s argue quite strongly that the self-conscious organization of white ethnics on the basis of their ethnicity was a racist response to the civil rights movement of the 1960s and 1970s and to celebrations of racial and ethnic identities by non-white groups.

Michael Novak, author of *The Rise of the Unmeltable Ethnics*, was the conservative leader of the white ethnic movement of the 1970s. He tries to answer the criticism that white ethnics are anti-black and "going back to their ethnicity" in order to oppose the black power movement. He writes: "The new ethnicity is the nation's best hope for confronting racial hatred. A Pole who knows he is a Pole, who is proud to be a Pole, who knows the social costs and possibilities of being a Polish worker in America, who knows where he stands in power, status and integrity—such a Pole can face a black militant eye to eye" (Novak 1973, 294). Novak really could not have been more wrong here, but not only for the most obvious reason. In the context of the content of the rest of his book and the debates of the early 1970s, Novak was wrong because the "new white ethnics" *were* in opposition to the black power movement, and various other developments that came out of the civil rights movement. And Novak's own work was read then and can be read now as fanning the flames of racial division at the time.

But the other sense in which Novak is wrong in this passage is in part a result of some of the developments of the new ethnicity movement of the 1970s. A Polish-American who "knows he is a Pole, who is proud to be a Pole, who knows the social costs and possibilities of being a Polish worker" is less able to understand the experience of being black in America precisely because of being "in touch with his own ethnicity." That is because the nature of being a Pole in America is as I have described it throughout this book—lacking in social costs, providing enjoyment, and chosen voluntarily.

One of the major points of this book has been the disparity between the idea and the reality of ethnicity for white ethnics. The reality is that white ethnics have a lot more choice and room for maneuver than they themselves think they do. The situation is very different for members of racial minorities, whose lives are strongly influenced by their race or national origin regardless of how much they may choose not to identify themselves in ethnic or racial terms. Yet my respondents did not make a distinction between their own

experience of ethnicity as a personal choice and the experience of
being a member of a racial minority.

People who assert a symbolic ethnicity do not give much attention
to the ease with which they are able to slip in and out of their ethnic
roles. It is quite natural to them that in the greater part of their lives,
their ethnicity does not matter. They also take for granted that when
it does matter, it is largely a matter of personal choice and a source of
pleasure.

The fact that ethnicity is something that is enjoyed and will not
cause problems for the individual is something people just accept.
This also leads to the belief that all ancestries are equal—more or less
interchangeable, but that you should be proud of and enjoy the one
you have. Louise Taylor articulated this attitude:

> You have to be something. I am sure I would be happy with whatever I
> was. It is like matter, mass, you have to come from somewhere. I could not
> imagine myself being unhappy with anything...I am sure if I was Swedish
> and Japanese combination...the feelings of happiness and self-esteem
> would be the same.

The sentiment among my respondents was that people should be
proud of their heritage, whatever it is. And because they happened to
be Irish or Polish or Italian, they were proud to be Irish or Italian or
Polish. But they could just as easily have been something different.
Ellen Albert:

> Q: Would you say that being Irish is important to you now?
>
> A: Well, I don't know. I have fun being it. I would not know what to say.
>   I have never been anything else. I am proud of it, but I am not really
>   100 percent anyway. And my husband, he doesn't have a drop in him
>   and you should see him on Saint Patrick's Day.

This approach to their own ethnicity leads to a situation where
whites with a symbolic ethnicity are unable to understand the everyday influence and importance of skin color and racial minority status
for members of minority groups in the United States. This lack of
understanding of the difference between the experience of ethnicity
for white Americans and the implications of ethnicity for members of
racial minorities was made quite clear in an interchange in the "Dear
Abby" newspaper column. The following debate is between two
Irish-Americans and two Asian-Americans on the issue of whether or
not it is polite to inquire about an individual's ethnic background. The

Irish-Americans cannot understand why the Asian-Americans are offended:

Dear Abby,

   Regarding "100 Percent American," the American of Oriental descent who complained that within five minutes of being introduced to a Caucasian, he was asked, "What are you?": You replied that it was rude to ask personal questions at any time, but because the average Caucasian doesn't know a Chinese from a Japanese, Cambodian, Vietnamese, Korean or a Thai, the question seemed reasonable—but it was still rude.

   Rude? I disagree. Inquiries about a person's roots are not necessarily rude. It shows a sincere interest in their heritage.

   The Orient is a rich and diverse geography. The face of an Oriental reveals his heritage. His looks tell of a passage through villages, cultures and languages—but which ones? His story is probably quite fascinating. I don't think it is rude to observe that such a face has a rich ancestry. I think it is a positive component of international understanding.

                                                     AN AMERICAN NAMED FINN

Abby replied:

My mail was heavy on this one. Without exception, all writers of Oriental descent resented being asked, "What are you?" shortly after being introduced. A typical letter:

Dear Abby,

   I, too, am 100 percent American and because I am of Asian ancestry, I am often asked, "What are you?" It's not the personal nature of this question that bothers me, it's the question itself. This query seems to question my very humanity. "What am I?" Why I am a person like everyone else!

   Another question I am frequently asked is, "Where did you come from?" This would be an innocent question, when one Caucasian asks it of another, but when it is asked of an Asian, it takes on a different tone...

                                                     A REAL AMERICAN

Dear Abby,

   Why do people resent being asked what they are? The Irish are so proud of being Irish, they tell you before you even ask. Tip O'Neill has never tried to hide his Irish ancestry.

                                                     JIMMY

(*San Francisco Chronicle*, February 28, 1986)

I was struck when I read this by how well it summarized the ways in which I found that the symbolic ethnicity of my respondents related to their ideas about racial minorities in our society. "An American

Named Finn" cannot understand why Asians are not as happy to be asked about their ancestry as he is because he understands his ethnicity and theirs to be separate but equal. Everyone has to come from somewhere—his family from Ireland, another's family from Asia—each has a history and each should be proud of it. But the reason he cannot understand the perspective of the Asian-American is that all ethnicities are not equal, all are not symbolic, costless, and voluntary. And that is where the subtle effect of symbolic ethnicity on American race relations develops.

The people I interviewed were not involved in ethnic organizations and were not self-consciously organized on the basis of their ethnicity. However, I do think that the way they experience their ethnicity creates a climate leading to a lack of understanding of the ethnic or racial experience of others. People equated their European ancestral background with the backgrounds of people from minority groups and saw them as interchangeable.

Thus respondents told me they just did not see why blacks and Mexican-Americans were always blaming things on their race or their ethnicity. For instance, Bill McGowan:

> A lot of people have problems that they bring on themselves. I don't care what religion or what nationality they are. The Mexicans, a lot of times they will say, "Well, it is because I am Mexican that it is much harder." But if they were Irish they might have the same problems. People are people.

Barbara Richter:

> I think black people still do face discrimination to a point. But when other people come to this country with half a brain in their head and some industrious energy and they make it on their own after a while, I just think the opportunities are there for everyone.

Sean O'Brien:

> I think everybody has the same opportunity. It doesn't matter what their background is. The education is there and if they have the gumption to go after it, they can do anything they damn well please. It doesn't make any difference if they are Irish, German, Jewish, Italian, or black. There are all different groups who are multi-millionaires. They have the same opportunities. I think a black kid has the same opportunity as one of my own.

Tim McDaniel:

> I think black people and Hispanic people face discrimination. Definitely. I think a lot of it they bring on themselves. They talk too much about it. If they would let it go it would be better.

Others denied, especially, that blacks were experiencing discrimination, citing examples of when affirmative action policies had hurt them or their families as "reverse discrimination." Megan O'Keefe:

> I never saw blacks being discriminated against at all. Now whether they are or not, maybe it is true. But I have seen a lot of the reverse. I have seen a lot of reverse discrimination.

Part of the tradition handed down as part of an ethnic ancestry are the family stories about ancestors having faced discrimination in the past. In fact, a large part of what people want to pass on to their children is the history of discrimination and struggle that ancestors faced when first arriving in the United States. All of my respondents were sure that their ancestors had faced discrimination when they first came to the United States. Many had heard stories about it within their families, some had read about it in history books, but all were sure it had happened. It was also one of the most important things mentioned to me by parents when they talked about what they wanted their children to know about their ethnic ancestry. For instance, Elaine Williams wanted her children to know about the hardships associated with their Italian ancestry:

> I just want them to know who they are and appreciate where they came from. I like them to talk to my older aunts. Sometimes they will tell them stories about when they were in Italy. Things like that. Because I don't think my kids know any hardship. Not that I know a lot, but I think it is nice to know the things people went through to put you where you are.

This is interesting, because Elaine herself did not think that her family had experienced much hardship until her father told her some stories one day at dinner:

> About four or five months ago we had a discussion at dinner about this. I had said that I never thought I had been prejudiced against because I was Italian. My dad went into a tirade about how back then it was much more common. He told us about different things that happened to him and just the general attitude toward Italians. It kind of stunned me because I had never experienced that. But my dad says that just because I didn't live through it, I should know that there was more anti-Italian feelings back when he was younger.

Most people had heard stories about how their ancestors had faced discrimination in the past. Rich Cahill, a 29-year-old policeman, described what he had heard in his family: "I know my grandmother used to tell me that there used to be signs in different places saying 'Irish need not apply.' In Philadelphia and down at the shore." Judy Gilligan spoke of the problem faced by her Serbian ancestors: "They talked about fights they had with other kids on the street, and being called guinea, honky. Those kinds of names. My grandparents told me the stories about how during the depression their milk box would be raided. People would come steal their milk."

People were all aware of the fact that their ancestors had come here as immigrants to make a better life and that they had faced adversity to do it—and they often pointed to the similarities between the experience of their ancestors and the discrimination experienced by non-whites now. Carol Davis's image of what it used to be like for the Irish is perhaps the most affected by being seen through the prism of the civil rights movement:

Q: Did your ancestors face discrimination when they first came here?

A: Yes, from what I was told they were. I know that Irish people were treated almost like blacks for a while. They weren't allowed in certain buildings. They were discriminated against. From what my mother says there were even signs in Philadelphia for Irish people not to come into the restaurants. I think they were even forced to ride in the back of the bus for a while there.

This type of interpretation of history contributes to the problems middle-class Americans of European origin have in understanding the experiences of their contemporary non-white fellow citizens.[3] The idea that the Irish were forced to sit at the back of a bus (when, in 1840?) in a sense could be seen to bring people together. The message of such a belief is that all ethnicities are similar and all will eventually end up successful. If the Irish had to sit at the back of the bus sometime in the past, and now being Irish just means having fun at funerals, then there is hope for all groups facing discrimination now. But, of course, if the Irish did not need legislation to allow them into

---

3. I do not want to minimize the Irish experience of discrimination and hostility in America in the mid-to-late nineteenth century. There was a great deal of anti-Irish feeling and discrimination, especially in Boston, New York, and other East Coast cities. However, the negative experiences of the Irish were never as extreme or as long lived as the discrimination and violence experienced by blacks and American Indians. (For detailed discussions of the different experiences of America's white and non-white groups see Lieberson 1980 and Blauner 1972.) In the case of Carol Davis's understanding of this situation, it is clear that she is interpreting her knowledge of the experiences of discrimination of the American Irish through her experience of the civil rights movement of American blacks.

the front of the bus, then why do blacks? If the Irish could triumph over hardships and discrimination through individual initiative and hard work, then why the need for affirmative action and civil rights legislation?

It is clear that people have a sense that being an immigrant was hard, that society did not accept their groups, and that now discrimination and prejudice is much less than it was before. People also believe that blacks, Hispanics, and Asians are still in a somewhat earlier stage. But, on the other hand, beliefs that the discrimination faced by Irish, Italians, and Serbs was the same both in degree and in kind as that faced by non-whites sets the stage for resentment of any policies that single out racial minorities.

The way in which they think about their own ethnicity—the voluntary, enjoyable aspects of it—makes it difficult to understand the contemporary position of non-whites. Thus some people made it a point to assert their ethnic identity on forms or in situations where forms or institutions were trying to determine minority status. For instance, Patrick O'Connor answered that he would put "Irish" as his answer to the ancestry question on the census form. But then he volunteered that that is not the only place he puts "Irish": "In fact, I put 'Irish' on all sorts of forms when they ask for racial identity. They want black or white, I always put 'Irish.' Let them figure out what it means." Lisa Paulo also gives her ethnicity on forms she knows are not specifically asking for it:

> On those forms it usually is, "Oh, you are Portuguese," therefore you have to be white Caucasian and so it usually gets pushed aside. And I usually feel more upset that it gets pushed aside than anything else. If you have a special category for Afro-American and for Filipino-American why can't you have one for Portuguese? I will mark "Other" and then just write in "Portuguese," because I get tired of being white Caucasian.

But most respondents no longer saw their ethnicity as having that much influence on their lives anymore. For most people I spoke with, ethnicity is something everyone has to have, but why would people be particularly proud of their ethnic ancestry or ashamed of it? It is just something you have, not something that really influences your life. Most respondents would admit that there was something different about blacks, Hispanics, and Asians, that they had faced some societal discrimination, especially in the past, but in another sense the individualistic approach to ethnicity was a much stronger influence. Some people stressed that they thought all societal discrimination against blacks and Hispanics had lessened to the point where they should just start forgetting about it and act as individuals, not as groups. In short, if your own ethnicity is a voluntaristic personal matter, it is sometimes difficult to understand that race or ethnicity for others is influenced by societal and political components.

In this sense the process and content of symbolic ethnicity tend to reinforce one another. If invoking an ethnic background is increasingly a voluntary, individual decision, and if it is understood that invoking that background is done for the enjoyment of the personality traits or rituals that one associates with one's ethnicity, then ethnicity itself takes on certain individual and positive connotations. The process and content of a symbolic ethnicity then make it increasingly difficult for white ethnics to sympathize with or understand the experience of a non-symbolic ethnicity—the experience of racial minorities in the United States.

THE FUTURE OF SYMBOLIC ETHNICITY

This analysis suggests both that symbolic ethnicity persists because it meets a need Americans have for community without individual cost and that a potential societal cost of this symbolic ethnicity is in its subtle reinforcement of racism. Perhaps this is an inherent danger in any pluralist society. The celebration of the fact that we all have heritages implies an equality among those heritages. This would obscure the fact that the experiences of non-whites have been qualitatively and quantitatively different from those of whites.

It is true that at the turn of the century Italians were considered by some to be non-whites. It is also true that there were signs in many East Coast cities prohibiting the Irish from applying for jobs or entering establishments. The discrimination faced by Jews was even greater. They were excluded from certain neighborhoods, organizations, and occupations. Yet the degree of discrimination against white European immigrants and their children never matched the systematic, legal and official discrimination and violence experienced by blacks, Hispanics, and Asians in America. The fact that whites of European ancestry today can enjoy an ethnicity that gives them options and brings them enjoyment with little or no social cost is no small accomplishment. But does it mean that in time we shall have a pluralist society with symbolic ethnicity for all Americans?

The respondents described in this study are socially mobile, middle-class whites, and their type of ethnic identity is specific to their social situation. As the description of the experiences of southern and eastern European immigrants at the beginning of the book suggests, the experience of ethnicity would have been very different at the turn of the century. This is a crucial aspect of ethnicity that is important to remember—ethnicity is historically variable. In the past it had social costs associated with it for these white groups. It has few, if any, now.

However, this symbolic ethnicity is not just something associated with generational movement. It is also very much dependent on social mobility. As long as racial or ethnic identity is associated with class stratification, or as long as ascriptive characteristics are used to assign rewards in society, ethnic identity will be much more complex than individual choice and selective personal and familial enjoyment of tradition.

The effects of changes in American immigration law make it difficult at times to distinguish developments owing to generational mobility from those owing to social and economic mobility. This is because the social and economic mobility of white ethnics in the twentieth century coincided with the drastic reduction in immigration from European sources—which means that the cohorts of Poles and Italians advancing socially and generationally have not been followed by large numbers of fresh immigrants who take over unskilled jobs and populate ethnic ghettos. Thus when the socially mobile children and grandchildren of the original immigrants left the urban ghettos and unskilled jobs for college and the suburbs in the 1950s and 1960s, blacks, Hispanics, and Asians took their places. The social mobility that makes a symbolic ethnicity possible for these whites might have looked very different if the supply of new immigrants from Europe had not been drastically curtailed.

This also makes it difficult to generalize from the experience of these white ethnic groups to the experiences of the largely non-European immigrants arriving since the 1965 immigration law. There is definitely evidence of social mobility and increasing intermarriage among the second- and among the small number of third-generation Asian-Americans. There is also evidence of social mobility and intermarriage among Hispanics. However, both of these groups are different from groups of European origin in that there is a continuing supply of new immigrants who take the place of the older generations in the ethnic neighborhoods and occupations. Middle-class third-generation Mexican-Americans may enjoy some of the same intermittent and voluntary aspects of ethnic identity as Italian-Americans, but the existence of a strong first-generation ethnic community, as well as of continued discrimination in housing and employment against Hispanics, would probably impose constraints on such upwardly mobile third-generation Mexican-Americans that it would not on Italian-Americans.

Aside from the very crucial issue of eradicating racial discrimination—which is still an inescapable fact of life for those of non-European descent in the United States—the question of the development of this type of symbolic ethnicity among these new immigrant groups is open because of the fact that they are at the forefront of a still-active immigrant stream. As these new groups—such as Chinese, Koreans, Jamaicans, and Filipinos—move into the third generation and into middle-class suburbs, more studies such as this one should be done on the later-generation form of ethnicity.

Given the fact that the structural conditions and trends that give rise to symbolic ethnicity are continuing, I would expect that symbolic ethnicity will continue to characterize the ethnicity of later-generation whites. The individual and familial construction of the substance of that ethnicity, along with increasing intermarriage, means that the shared content of any one ethnicity will become even more diluted. Consequently there will be increased dependence on the mass media, ethnic stereotypes, and popular culture to tell people how to be Irish or Italian or Polish.

But that dilution of the content of ethnicity does not necessarily mean that there will be a decline in the personal satisfaction associated with having a symbolic ethnicity. Partly this is because the contentless nature of this ethnicity enables it to provide the feeling of community with no cost to the individuality we Americans value so highly. But it is also because this ethnicity is associated by people with close and intimate ties in their nuclear families, in fragments of their extended families, and with close friends and neighbors. The Saint Patrick's Day parties I attended with my respondents may not have had too much to do with being Irish, and the people giving them may have had very little Irish in their complicated family trees, but the parties were warm and rich celebrations, which embody traditions for the people who gather each year. The "community" that gathers for these celebrations is not necessarily illusory, but it is a voluntary, personally constructed, American creation.

The paradox of symbolic ethnicity is that it depends upon the ultimate goal of a pluralist society and at the same time makes it more difficult to achieve that ultimate goal. It is dependent upon the concept that all ethnicities mean the same thing—that enjoying the traditions of one's heritage is an option available to a group or individual—but that such a heritage should not have any social costs associated with it. The options of symbolic ethnicity involve choosing among elements in one's ancestry and choosing when and if voluntarily to enjoy the traditions of that ancestry. However, the interviews presented here show that the individuals who enjoy a symbolic ethnicity for themselves do not always recognize the options they enjoy or the ways in which their own concepts of ethnicity and uses of those concepts constrain and deny choice to others.

Americans who have a symbolic ethnicity continue to think of ethnicity—as well as race—as being biologically rooted. They enjoy many choices themselves, but they continue to ascribe identities to others—especially those they can identify by skin color. Thus a person with a black skin who had some Irish ancestry would have to work very hard to decide to present him or herself as Irish—and in many important ways he/she would be denied that option. The discussion of racial intermarriage makes this point clearly—racial identity is understood by these respondents as an inherited physical aspect of an individual, not as a social construct. Thus respondents exhibit contradictory ideas about minorities in American society—they are clear that there is a fundamental difference between a white ethnic and a black person when the issue is intermarriage in their own families. On the other hand, they do not understand why blacks seem to make such a big deal about their ethnicity. They see an equivalence between the African-American and, say, Polish-American heritages.

So symbolic ethnicity only works for some ancestries—the pluralist ideal of an equality of heritages is far from a reality in American life. But at the same time, as I have argued, the legacy of symbolic ethnicity is to imply that this equality exists. The political result of that ideological legacy is a backlash against affirmative action programs that recognize and try to redress the inequalities in our society.

The ultimate goal of a pluralist society should be a situation of symbolic ethnicity for all Americans. If all Americans were free to exercise their "ethnic option" with the certainty that there would be no costs associated with it, we could all enjoy the voluntary, pleasurable aspects of ethnic traditions in the way my respondents describe their own enjoyments. It is important not to romanticize the traditional white ethnic group. In addition to its positive aspects, it was experienced as extremely constricting and narrow by many people. There are parts of these past ethnic traditions that are sexist, racist, clannish, and narrow-minded. With a symbolic ethnic identity an individual can choose to celebrate an ethnic holiday and refuse to perpetuate a sexist tradition that values boys over girls or that channels girls into domestic roles without their consent. The selective aspects of a symbolic ethnicity are in part what make it so enjoyable to so many individuals.

Currently, however, we are far removed from a position where this freedom is available for all. As the Asian-Americans who wrote to Dear Abby make clear, there are many societal issues and involuntary ascriptions associated with non-white identities. The developments necessary for this to change are not individual but societal in nature. Social mobility and declining racial and ethnic sensitivity are closely associated. The legacy and the present reality of discrimination on the basis of race or ethnicity must be overcome before the ideal of a pluralist society where all heritages are treated equally and are equally available for individuals to choose or discard at will is realized. It is a sad irony that the enjoyment and individual character of their own ethnicity contributes to the thinking that makes these middle-class whites oppose the very programs designed to achieve that reality.

The 1980 Census
Ancestry Question

Facsimile of questionnaire item 14.

> **14. What is this person's ancestry?** *If uncertain about how to report ancestry, see instruction guide.*
>
> _____
>
> *(For example: Afro-Amer., English, French, German, Honduran, Hungarian, Irish, Italian, Jamaican, Korean, Lebanese, Mexican, Nigerian, Polish, Ukrainian, Venezuelan, etc.)*

Facsimile of instructions to the respondent for questionnaire item 14.

14. Print the ancestry group with which the person *identifies*. Ancestry (or origin or descent) may be viewed as the nationality group, the lineage, or the country in which the person or the person's parents or ancestors were born before their arrival in the United States. Persons who are of more than one origin and who cannot identify with a single group should print their multiple ancestry (for example, German-Irish).

Be specific; for example, if ancestry is "Indian," specify whether American Indian, Asian Indian, or West Indian. Distinguish Cape Verdean from Portuguese, and French Canadian from Canadian.

A religious group should not be reported as a person's ancestry.

SOURCE: Bureau of the Census 1980b.

169

Interview Questions

1. Begin with the census form from 1980. Show interviewee the ancestry question and instructions if they need them. How would you answer this question? Why?

2. Who in the house would have filled out the census form?

3. How would the person who filled out the census form (if different from interviewee) have filled out the census form?

4. List other people in the household. What would have been the ancestry response for them?

5. Family history. Parents. Grandparents and as far back as the interviewee can remember.

Who in your family were the original immigrants?

Where did they come from?

How long ago did they come here?

How old were they when they immigrated?

Do you know why they left?

Why did they choose the United States?

Where did they settle?

Occupation, education?

Did their whole family come over or just them?

How do you know this information?

For each parent, grandparent, child, brother, and sister of the interviewee collect information on:

occupation

education

location

6.   What is your religion? Were you raised in it? About how often would you estimate that you attend religious services?

7.   Did you speak a language other than English at home growing up? How much was spoken, where and by whom? Did your parents, grandparents?

8.   Do you speak a language other than English at home now? How often? On what occasions?

9.   Where were you born?

10.   Where did you grow up?

11.   Where else did you live?

12.   How long have you lived in the area you live in now?

13.   Have you moved in the last five years?

14.   What was the most common ethnicity in the neighborhood where you grew up?

15.   Could you estimate what percent of the population was that ethnicity?

16.   When you were growing up did you consider yourself ethnic (a member of an ethnic group)?

17.   Did you grow up in an ethnic neighborhood? friends, neighbors members of your ethnic group?

18.   Were there any other ethnic groups around when you were growing up?

19.   How different were they from your ethnic group?

20.   How did your parents feel about their ethnic background?

21.   Did they talk about it often?

22.   Did they belong to any ethnic organizations or clubs?

23. Was it important to you or to your parents for you to date someone of your own ethnic group?

24. Did you ever go out with someone who was not from your ethnic group?

25. Did you ever go out with someone who was from your ethnic group?

26. If yes, how did your parents react? How did your friends react?

27. Did you marry someone from the same ethnic ancestry?

28. If not, do you think it would have been possible for you to marry someone outside the ethnic group or would your parents have objected?

29. What about outside of your religion? Do you think both of these things were equally important to your parents?

30. Did any of your brothers and sisters or aunts or uncles marry outside your ethnic group? How was this seen by the rest of the family? How did they treat them?

31. Are family values different for (name ethnic group)? In what way?

ETHNIC IDENTITY

32. Is it a common occurrence for people to ask or comment on your ethnic background? Can you recall the last time someone asked or commented on it?

33. Do you belong to any ethnic organizations or clubs? What do they do there?

34. Do you belong to any other organizations or clubs?

35. Would you say that being —— is important to you?

36. Can you think of times in your life that it has been more or less important?

37. Have there been any specific times you feel you have benefited from being ——? Can you recall the last time?

38. Have you ever felt any personal discrimination or hostility in getting a house or apartment? Getting a job or a promotion? In any other way?

39. Can you recall the last time?

40. Do you know of any people who have changed their name? What do you think of this practice?

41. Do jokes about —— bother you? Does it matter whether they are told by an —— or an outsider? Do you ever tell ——? Do you ever tell jokes about members of other ethnic groups?

42. Is there such a thing as an —— -American character? What do you think of when you think of someone as ——?

43. What are the traits of —— -Americans that you think are the best, the worst?

44. Is there any ethnic group you think is close to ——? Who? In what way are they close?

45. Do you think Americans have a stereotype of what being —— is? What is it?

46. Is there any validity to it? Where do you think this stereotype comes from?

47. I am going to ask you a really speculative question: if you could be a member of any ethnic group you wanted, which one would you choose? Why?

48. Do you have an idea of what Italians are like? (Ask of all groups). Where do those ideas come from? What do you think about them?

49. Have you ever visited the country any of your ancestors came from? Do you want to visit there?

50. Who do you root for in the Olympics?

51. Do you know where in —— your ancestors are from? How do you know this information?

52. Do you think of yourself as an American sometimes and as an —— other times? When does this happen? Can you give me an example of when being an American has been important to you? Are there any times when being —— is more important than being American?

53. Do you think there ever could be a time when being an American and being an —— could be in opposition?

54. What ethnic groups are your closest friends from?

55. I am going to ask you about some people who you might have ongoing contact with, could you tell me the ethnic ancestry and religion of all of these people?

Doctor

Dentist

Lawyer

Clergyman

56. Do you feel more comfortable being around —— than non- ——? At what times? Any idea why?

57.   Is your neighborhood characterized by a particular ethnic group? If so, what is it? If not, do you think you are missing something?

58.   If you moved somewhere new would you try to find some ——?

59.   How would you go about trying to find ——?

60.   Do you feel more comfortable with Catholics than with non-Catholics?

61.   Would you describe funerals in your family for me? What happens at them? Have you been to many funerals? How about weddings?

62.   Is there anything distinctive about —— weddings (that you have noticed is different from other people's ways of celebrating these)?

funerals?

christenings?

63.   Can you describe some of the —— customs or practices that affect your everyday life? i.e. food, music, cultural events?

64.   Do you eat any ethnic foods regularly?

65.   What are the holidays which you and your family celebrate that are the most important?

66.   Are there any family traditions you follow on Christmas, Easter?

67.   Are there any special holidays that you celebrate in a special way due to being ——?

68.   Have you ever done work in a political campaign? For whom, what did you do?

69.   When you decide who to vote for, does being an —— ever influence you?

70.   (If they have children) How important is being —— to your children?

71.   Do you think it is more or less important to them now? Why?

72.   Are any of your children married? To what ethnic group?

73.   What would you hope your grandchildren learn about being?

74.   Would you prefer your children to marry within their ethnicity, religion? race? Why?

75.   Would you describe yourself as working class, middle class, or upper class?

76.   What do you think most —— people are?

77. Do you think that there are major differences among ethnic groups in the U.S.?

78. Do you think your ancestors faced discrimination when they first came here?

79. Are there any nationality or religious groups that you think face discrimination now?

80. Do you think that the public schools should teach more about the contribution of ―― to American life?

81. What do you think of bilingual education in the nation's schools?

82. Do you think there is an American national character? Do you exhibit those traits? What are they?

83. Will you try (or have you tried) to tell your children about the mix of ethnic groups in your family background?

DEMOGRAPHICS

1. What year were you born?

2. What is your occupation?

3. What is the highest grade of school you completed? Was any of it in parochial school?

Respondents

California Sample

Name	Sex	Age	Occupation	Education	Generation	Ethnicity
Ellen Albert	F	58	housewife	12 yrs.	4th (2d)	Irish-French
Robert Albert	M	60	shipping clerk	12 yrs.	3d	Italian
Susan Badovich	F	29	librarian	B.A.	3d	Slovenian
Helen Binet	F	56	housewife	12 yrs.	3d	German-Irish-Welsh
Paul Binet	M	57	engineer	M.A.	unk	Scots-Welsh
Terry Binet	F	29	computer programmer	M.A.	4th	German-Irish-Scots-Welsh
Dan Burke	M	26	lawyer	law	4th	Irish-Norwegian-Dutch-English-French-American Indian
Anne Campbell	F	20	student	14 yrs.	3d	Irish-Scots
Anne Gold	F	52	x-ray technician	12 yrs.	4th	Irish-English
Mike Gold	M	54	lawyer	law	4th	English-French-Polish
Laurie Jablonski	F	29	social worker	M.A.	4th	German-Polish-English
Bill Kerrigan	M	19	student	14 yrs.	3d	Irish-German-French
Bill McGowan	M	62	retired army officer	12 yrs.	3d	Irish
Mary McGowan	F	60	day care	12 yrs.	3d	Irish
Christine O'Brien	F	47	nurse	B.A.	3d	Irish-Italian
Sean O'Brien	M	52	golf pro	12 yrs.	3d	Irish-Scots
Patrick O'Connor	M	26	student	B.A.	5th	Irish
Bonnie Ostrowski	F	50	housewife	B.A.	2d	Polish
Stan Ostrowski	M	55	mechanic	B.A.	4th	Polish-German-Scots-Irish
Lisa Paulo	F	24	bank teller	B.A.	3d	Portuguese
Janet Albert Parro	F	28	housewife	12 yrs.	4th	Irish-Italian-French
Maria Reggio	F	46	housewife	12 yrs.	2d	Italian
Greg Reggio	M	48	fireman	12 yrs.	3d	Portuguese
Barbara Richter	F	51	housewife	12 yrs.	4th	Irish
Ben Richter	M	56	telephone co. mgr.	B.A.	4th	Irish-French-German
Pete Scotto	M	20	student	14 yrs.	3d	Italian
Rose Scotto	F	53	housewife	12 yrs.	3d	Italian
Tom Scotto	M	60	iron worker	10 yrs.	2d	Italian
Father Pat Stevens	M	47	priest	M.A.	4th	Irish-German
Louise Taylor	F	26	engineer	B.A.	5th	Irish-Italian-Scots-English

Pennsylvania Sample

Name	Sex	Age	Occupation	Education	Generation	Ethnicity
Joe Bajko	M	20	college student	14 yrs.	3d	Lithuanian-Welsh-English
Suzanne Benson	F	47	clerk	B.A.	3d	Italian-Irish
Cindy Betz	F	26	student	B.A.	4th	Italian-Czech
Joan Cahill	F	24	account rep.	B.A.	3d	Irish
Rich Cahill	M	29	policeman	B.A.	3d	Irish
Carol Gilligan Davis	F	32	technical artist	12 yrs.	4th	Irish-British
John Davis	M	32	machinist	B.A.	4th	Irish-English-Czech
Antonio Donio	M	54	manager	B.A.	3d	Italian
Rosemary Donio	F	48	teacher	B.A.	3d	Irish
Liz Field	F	35	weaver	B.A.	5th	Scots-Irish-English-German-French
Judy Gilligan	F	44	stockbroker	M.A.	3d	Serbian-Welsh-English
Anne Greene	F	51	nurse	B.A.	3d	Polish-German
Joyce Hoffman	F	36	teacher	B.A.	4th	German-Scots-English
Anne Hogarty	F	51	housewife/realtor	B.A.	4th	Irish-Scots-Welsh
Bill Hogarty	M	52	lawyer	law	3d	French-Irish-Italian-Scots
Jim Hogarty	M	21	student	B.A.	4th	French-Irish-Italian-Scots
Ted Jackson	M	27	office worker	B.A.	4th	Irish-French-German-English-Scots
Kate McDaniel	F	64	housewife	12 yrs.	3d	Irish
Tim McDaniel	M	68	retired civil servant	B.A.	3d	Irish
Catherine Masden	F	27	paralegal	B.A.	3d	German-Swiss-Lithuanian
Steve Mason	M	67	retired	B.A.	4th	German-Italian-English
Betty O'Keefe	F	60	housewife	B.A.	5th	Irish-French
Jack O'Keefe	M	62	contractor	B.A.	4th	Irish
Megan O'Keefe	F	28	housewife	M.A.	4th	Irish
Mike O'Keefe	M	31	banker	B.A.	5th	Irish-French
Rose Peters	F	46	manager	B.A.	4th	Italian-Irish-Welsh-English-Lithuanian
Jeanne Robinson	F	34	teacher	M.A.	3d	Polish
Joe Robinson	M	36	computer programmer	M.A.	3d	Irish-Italian
Elaine Williams	F	32	student	B.A.	3d	Italian
Joe Williams	M	33	sales	B.A.	4th	German-Irish-Scots

Bibliography

Abramson, Harold J. 1971. "Inter-Ethnic Marriage among Catholic Americans and Changes in Religious Behavior." *Sociological Analysis* 32, no. 1:31–44.

——. 1973. *Ethnic Diversity in Catholic America*. New York: Wiley.

——. 1975. "The Religioethnic Factor and the American Experience: Another Look at the Third Generation Hypothesis." *Ethnicity* 2:163–77.

——. 1980. Assimilation and Pluralism. In *The Harvard Encyclopedia of Ethnic Groups*, ed. Stephen Thernstrom, 150–60. Cambridge, Mass.: Harvard University Press.

Agocs, Carol. 1981. "Ethnic Settlement in a Metropolitan Area: A Typology of Communities." *Ethnicity* 8:127–48.

Aguirre, B. E., Kent P. Schwirian, and Anthony J. LaGreca. 1980. "The Residential Patterning of Latin Americans and Other Ethnic Populations in Metropolitan Miami." *Latin American Research Review* 15:35–63.

Alba, Richard D. 1976. "Social Assimilation among American Catholic National Origin Groups." *American Sociological Review* 41, no. 6 (December): 1030–46.

——. 1978 "Ethnic Networks and Tolerant Attitudes." *Public Opinion Quarterly* 42, no. 1 (Spring): 1–16.

——. 1981. "The Twilight of Ethnicity among American Catholics of European Ancestry." *Annals of the American Academy of Political and Social Science* 454 (March): 86–97.

——. 1985a. "Interethnic and Interracial Marriage in the 1980 Census." Paper presented at the Annual Meeting of the American Sociological Association, Washington, D.C., 1985.

——. 1985b. *Italian Americans: Into the Twilight of Ethnicity*. Englewood Cliffs, N.J.: Prentice-Hall.

——. 1988. "Cohorts and the Dynamics of Ethnic Change." In *Social Structures and Human Lives*, ed. Matilda White Riley, Bettina J. Huber, and Beth B. Hess, 211–28. Beverly Hills, Calif.: Sage Publications.

——. 1990. *Ethnic Identity: The Transformation of Ethnicity in the Lives of Americans of European Ancestry*. New Haven: Yale University Press. Forthcoming.

Alba, Richard D., and Mitchell B. Chamlin. 1983. "A Preliminary Examination of Ethnic Identification among Whites." *American Sociological Review* 48, no. 2 (April): 240–47.

Alba, Richard D., and Reid M. Golden. 1984. "Patterns of Ethnic Marriage in the United States." Paper presented at the Annual Meeting of the American Sociological Association, San Antonio, Texas, 1984.

Alba, Richard D., and R. G. Kessler. 1979. "Patterns of Interethnic Marriage among Catholic Americans." *Social Forces* 57, no. 4 (June): 124–40.

Alba, Richard D., and Gwen Moore. 1982. "Ethnicity in the American Elite." *American Sociological Review* 47, no. 3 (June): 373–83.

Barth, Frederik, ed. 1969. *Ethnic Groups and Boundaries: The Social Organization of Culture Difference*. Boston: Little, Brown.

Bean, Frank D., and Marta Tienda. 1987. *The Hispanic Population of the United States*. New York: Russell Sage Foundation.

Beeman, William O. 1986. "Freedom to Choose: Symbols and Values in American Advertising." In *Symbolizing America*, ed. Herve Varenne, 52–65. Lincoln: University of Nebraska Press.

Bell, Daniel. 1975. "Ethnicity and Social Change." In *Ethnicity: Theory and Experience*, ed. N. Glazer and D. P. Moynihan, 141–74. Cambridge, Mass.: Harvard University Press.

Bellah, Robert, Richard Madsen, William M. Sullivan, Ann Swidler, and Steven M. Tipton. 1985. *Habits of the Heart: Individualism and Commitment in American Life*. Berkeley: University of California Press.

Blauner, Robert. 1972. *Racial Oppression in America*. New York: Harper & Row.

Bogardus, E. S. 1933. "A Social Distance Scale." *Sociology and Social Research* 17 (January–February): 265–71.

Bonacich, Edna. 1980. "Class Approaches to Ethnicity and Race." *Insurgent Sociologist* 10:2. Reprinted in *Majority and Minority: The Dynamics of Race and Ethnicity in American Life*, ed. Norman R. Yetman, 62–78. Newton, Mass.: Allyn & Bacon.

Bram, Joseph. 1965. "Change and Choice in Ethnic Identification." *Transactions of the New York Academy of Sciences*, 2d ser., 28:242–48.

Cohen, Steven M. 1977. "Socioeconomic Determinants of Intraethnic Marriage and Friendship." *Social Forces* 55, no. 4 (June): 997–1010.

Coleman, Richard P., and Lee Rainwater. 1978. *Social Standing in America: New Dimensions of Class*. New York: Basic Books.

Crispino, James A. 1980. *The Assimilation of Ethnic Groups: The Italian Case*. Staten Island, N.Y.: Center for Migration Studies.

Davis, James A., and Tom W. Smith. 1980a. *General Social Surveys: 1972–1980: Cumulative Codebooks*. Chicago: National Opinion Research Center.

———. 1980b. "Looking Backward: A National Sample Survey of Ancestors and Predecessors, 1980–1850." *Historical Methods* 13, no. 3 (Summer): 145–62.

di Leonardo, Micaela. 1984. *The Varieties of Ethnic Experience: Kinship, Class and Gender among Italian Americans.* Ithaca, N.Y.: Cornell University Press.

Dinnerstein, Leonard, and David M. Reimers. 1982. *Ethnic Americans: A History of Immigration and Assimilation.* New York: Harper & Row.

Fandetti, Donald V., and Donald E. Gelfand. 1983. "Middle Class White Ethnics in Suburbia: A Study of Italian-Americans." In *Culture, Ethnicity and Identity: Current Issues in Research*, ed. William C. McCready, 111–25. New York: Academic Press.

Farley, Reynolds, and Walter R. Allen. 1987. *The Color Line and the Quality of Life in America.* New York: Russell Sage Foundation.

Featherman, David L. 1971. "The Socioeconomic Achievement of White Religio-Ethnic Subgroups: Social and Psychological Explanations." *American Sociological Review* 36 (April): 207–22.

Friedman, Edwin H. 1982. "The Myth of the Shiksa." In *Ethnicity and Family Therapy*, ed. Monica McGoldrick et al., 499–526. New York: Guilford Press.

Gans, Herbert J. 1958. "The Origin and Growth of a Jewish Community in the Suburbs: A Study of the Jews of Park Forest." In *The Jews: Social Patterns of an American Group*, ed. Marshall Sklare, 205–48. Glencoe, Ill.: Free Press.

———. 1962. *The Urban Villagers.* Glencoe, Ill.: Free Press.

———. 1967. *The Levittowners: Ways of Life and Politics in a New Suburban Community.* New York: Pantheon Books.

———. 1979. "Symbolic Ethnicity: The Future of Ethnic Groups and Cultures in America." *Ethnic and Racial Studies* 2 (January): 1–20.

Glazer, Nathan, and Daniel Patrick Moynihan. 1963. *Beyond the Melting Pot: The Negroes, Puerto Ricans, Jews, Italians and Irish of New York City.* Cambridge, Mass.: MIT Press.

———. eds. 1975. *Ethnicity: Theory and Experience.* Cambridge, Mass.: Harvard University Press.

Gleason, Philip. 1980. American Identity and Americanization. In *The Harvard Encyclopedia of American Ethnic Groups*, ed. Stephen Thernstrom, 31–58. Cambridge, Mass.: Harvard University Press.

Goering, John M. 1971. "The Emergence of Ethnic Interests: A Case of Serendipity." *Social Forces* 48 (March): 379–84.

Gordon, Milton M. 1954. "Social Structure and Goals in Group Relations." In *Freedom and Control in Modern Society*, ed. Monroe Berger et al., 141–57. New York: D. Van Nostrand.

———. 1964. *Assimilation in American Life: The Role of Race, Religion, and National Origins.* New York: Oxford University Press.

———. 1981. "Models of Pluralism: The New American Dilemma." *Annals of the American Academy of Political and Social Science* 454 (March): 178–88.

Greeley, Andrew M. 1971. *Why Can't They Be Like Us: America's White Ethnic Groups.* New York: E. P. Dutton.

——. 1974. *Ethnicity in the United States: A Preliminary Reconaissance.* New York: Wiley.

——. 1976. "The Ethnic Miracle. *The Public Interest* 45 (Fall): 20–36.

——. 1976, *Ethnicity, Denomination, and Inequality.* Beverly Hills, Calif.: Sage Publications.

Greeley, Andrew M., and William C. McCready. 1975. "The Transmission of Cultural Heritages: The Case of the Irish and the Italians." In *Ethnicity: Theory and Experience,* ed. N. Glazer and D. P. Moynihan, 209–35. Cambridge, Mass.: Harvard University Press.

Guest, Avery M., and James A. Weed. 1976. "Ethnic Residential Segregation: Patterns of Change." *American Journal of Sociology* 81, no. 5 (March): 1088–1111.

Hansen, Marcus L. 1952. "The Third Generation in America." *Commentary* 14 (November): 492–500.

Hechter, Michael. 1974. "The Political Economy of Ethnic Change." *American Journal of Sociology* 79, no. 5 (March): 1151–78.

——. 1978. "Group Formation and the Cultural Division of Labor." *American Journal of Sociology* 84, no. 2 (September): 293–318.

——. 1983. "The Position of Eastern European Immigrants to the United States in the Cultural Division of Labor: Some Trends and Prospects." In *The Dynamics of East European Ethnicity outside of Eastern Europe,* ed. I. Winner and R. Susel, 185–206. Cambridge, Mass.: Schenkman Publishing.

Heer, David. M. 1980. "Intermarriage." In *The Harvard Encyclopedia of American Ethnic Groups,* ed. Stephen Thernstrom, 513–21. Cambridge, Mass.: Harvard University Press.

Herberg, Will. 1955. *Protestant, Catholic, Jew: An Essay in American Religious Sociology.* Chicago: University of Chicago Press.

Hirshman, Charles. 1983. "America's Melting Pot Reconsidered." *Annual Review of Sociology* 9:397–423.

Horowitz, Donald L. 1975. "Ethnic Identity." In *Ethnicity: Theory and Experience,* ed. N. Glazer and D. P. Moynihan, 111–40. Cambridge, Mass.: Harvard University Press.

Howe, Irving. 1977. "The Limits of Ethnicity." *New Republic* 18 (June 25): 17–19.

Hoyt, Danny R., and Nicholas Babchuk. 1981. "Ethnicity and the Voluntary Associations of the Aged." *Ethnicity* 8:67–81.

Isaacs, Harold R. 1975. "Basic Group Identity: Idols of the Tribe." In *Ethnicity: Theory and Experience,* ed. N. Glazer and D. P. Moynihan, 29–52. Cambridge, Mass.: Harvard University Press.

Johnson, Charles E., Jr. 1974. *Consistency of Reporting of Ethnic Origin in the Current Population Survey.* Bureau of the Census Technical Paper 31. Washington, D.C.: Government Printing Office.

Johnson, Colleen Leahy. 1985. *Growing Up and Growing Old in Italian-American Families.* New Brunswick, N.J.: Rutgers University Press.

Kantrowitz, Nathan. 1973. *Ethnic and Racial Segregation in the New York Metropolis: Residential Patterns among White Ethnic Groups, Blacks and Puerto Ricans*. New York: Praeger.

Kennedy, Ruby Jo Reeves. 1952. "Single or Triple Melting Pot? Intermarriage Trends in New Haven, 1870–1950." *American Journal of Sociology* 58 (July): 56–59.

Lazerwitz, Bernard, and Louis Rowitz. 1964. "The Three Generations Hypothesis." *American Journal of Sociology* 69 (March): 529–38.

Lieberson, Stanley. 1962. "Suburbs and Ethnic Residential Patterns." *American Journal of Sociology* 67 (May): 673–81.

——. 1963. *Ethnic Patterns in American Cities*. New York: Free Press.

——. 1980. *A Piece of the Pie: Blacks and White Immigrants since 1880*. Berkeley: University of California Press.

——. 1982. "Stereotypes: Their Consequences for Race and Ethnic Interaction." In *Social Structure and Behavior: Essays in Honor of William Hamilton Sewell*, 47–68. New York: Academic Press.

——. 1985. "Unhyphenated Whites in the United States." *Ethnic and Racial Studies* 8 (January): 159–80.

Lieberson, Stanely, and Lawrence Santi. 1985. "The Use of Nativity Data to Estimate Ethnic Characteristics and Patterns." *Social Science Research* 14, no. 1 (March): 31–56.

Lieberson, Stanley, and Mary C. Waters. 1985. "Ethnic Mixtures in the United States." *Sociology and Social Research* 70, no. 1 (October): 567–76.

——. 1986. "Ethnic Groups in Flux: The Changing Ethnic Responses of American Whites." *Annals of the American Academy of Political and Social Science* 487 (September): 79–91.

——. 1988. *From Many Strands: Ethnic and Racial Groups in Contemporary America*. New York: Russell Sage Foundation.

Lopata, Helen Znaniecki. 1976. *Polish Americans: Status Competition in an Ethnic Community*. Englewood Cliffs, N.J.: Prentice-Hall.

McGoldrick, Monica. 1982. "Irish Families." In *Ethnicity and Family Therapy*, ed. Monica McGoldrick et al., 310–39. New York: Guilford Press.

McGoldrick, Monica, John K. Pearce, and Joseph Giordano, eds. 1982. *Ethnicity and Family Therapy*. New York: Guilford Press.

McKay, James, and Frank Lewins. 1978. "Ethnicity and the Ethnic Group: A Conceptual Analysis and Reformulation." *Ethnic and Racial Studies* 1, no. 4 (October): 412–27.

Martinelli, Phylis Cancilla. 1983. "Beneath the Surface: Ethnic Communities in Phoenix, Arizona." In *Culture, Ethnicity and Identity: Current Issues in Research*, ed. William McCready, 181–94. New York: Academic Press.

Massey, Douglas S. 1985. "Ethnic Residential Segregation: A Theoretical Synthesis and Empirical Review." *Sociology and Social Research* 69, no. 3 (April): 315–50.

Mead, Margaret. 1975. "Ethnicity and Anthropology in America." In *Ethnic Identity: Cultural Continuities and Change*, ed. George De Vos and Lola Romanucci-Ross, 173–97. Palo Alto, Calif.: Mayfield Publishing Co.

Moitoza, Everett. 1982. "Portuguese Families." In *Ethnicity and Family Therapy*, ed. Monica McGoldrick et al., 412–31. New York: Guilford Press.

Mondykowski, Sandra M. 1982. "Polish Families." In *Ethnicity and Family Therapy*, ed. Monica McGoldrick et al., 393–411. New York: Guilford Press.

Nahirny, V., and J. A. Fishman. 1965. "American Immigrant Groups: Ethnic Identification and the Problem of Generations." *Sociological Review* 13:311–26.

Neidert, Lisa J., and Reynolds Farley. 1985. "Assimilation in the United States: An Analysis of Ethnic and Generation Differences in Status and Achievement." *American Sociological Review* 50, no. 6 (December): 840–50.

Novak, Michael. 1973. *The Rise of the Unmeltable Ethnics: Politics and Culture in the Seventies*. New York: Macmillan Co.

Okamura, Jonathan. 1981. "Situational Ethnicity." *Ethnic and Racial Studies* 4, no. 4 (October): 452–65.

Owen, Carolyn A., Howard C. Elsner, and Thomas R. McFaul. 1981. "A Half Century of Social Distance Research: National Replication of the Bogardus Studies." *Social Science Research* 66 (October): 80–95.

Paden, John N. 1967. "Situational Ethnicity in Urban Africa with Special Reference to the Hausa." Paper presented at African Studies Association Meeting in New York, November 1967.

Padgett, Deborah. 1980. "Symbolic Ethnicity and Patterns of Ethnic Identity Assertion in American-born Serbs." *Ethnic Groups* 3, no. 1 (December): 55–77.

Parenti, Michael. 1967. "Ethnic Politics and the Persistence of Ethnic Identification." *American Political Science Review* 61:717–26.

Park, Robert Ezra. 1950. *Race and Culture*. New York: Free Press.

Park, Robert E., Ernest W. Burgess, and Roderick D. McKenzie. *The City*. Chicago: University of Chicago Press.

Parsons, Talcott. 1975. "Some Theoretical Considerations on the Nature and Trends of Change in Ethnicity." In *Ethnicity: Theory and Experience*, ed. N. Glazer and D. P. Moynihan, 53–83. Cambridge, Mass.: Harvard University Press.

Patterson, Orlando. 1977. *Ethnic Chauvinism: The Reactionary Impulse*. New York: Stein & Day.

Pavalko, R. M. 1980. "Racism and the New Immigration: A Reinterpretation of Assimilation of White Ethnics in American Society." *Sociology and Social Research* 65, no. 1 (October): 56–77.

Peach, Ceri. 1980. "Which Triple Melting Pot? A Reexamination of Ethnic Intermarriage in New Haven, 1900–1950." *Ethnic and Racial Studies* 3, no. 1 (January): 1–16.

Peterson, William. 1980. "Concepts of Ethnicity." In *The Harvard Encyclopedia of American Ethnic Groups*, ed. Stephen Thernstrom, 234–42. Cambridge, Mass.: Harvard University Press.

Porter, John. 1975. "Ethnic Pluralism in Canadian Perspective." In *Ethni-*

city: Theory and Experience, ed. N. Glazer and D. P. Moynihan, 267–304. Cambridge, Mass.: Harvard University Press.

Reitz, Jeffrey G. 1980. *The Survival of Ethnic Groups.* Toronto: McGraw-Hill.

Reider, Jonathan. 1985. *Canarsie: The Jews and Italians of Brooklyn against Liberalism.* Cambridge, Mass.: Harvard University Press.

Riesman, David, Nathan Glazer, and Reuel Denney. 1950. *The Lonely Crowd: A Study of the Changing American Character.* New Haven, Conn.: Yale University Press.

Roche, John Patrick. 1984. "Social Factors Affecting Cultural, National and Religious Ethnicity: A Study of Suburban Italian Americans." *Ethnic Groups* 6, no. 1 (June): 27–45.

Roof, W. C. 1979. "Socioeconomic Differentials among White Socioreligious Groups in the United States." *Social Forces* 58, no. 1 (September): 280–89.

Ross, Edward Alsworth. 1914. *The Old World in the New.* New York: Century Co.

Rotunno, Marie, and Monica McGoldrick. 1982. "Italian Families." In *Ethnicity and Family Therapy,* ed. Monica McGoldrick et al., 340–63. New York: Guilford Press.

Royce, Anya P. 1982. *Ethnic Identity: Strategies of Diversity.* Bloomington: Indiana University Press.

Russo, N. J. 1969. "Three Generations of Italians in New York City: Their Religious Acculturation." *International Migration Review* 3 (Spring): 3–16.

Ryan, Joseph A., ed. 1973. *White Ethnics: Their Life in Working Class America.* Englewood Cliffs, N. J.: Prentice-Hall.

Schneider, David M. 1968. *American Kinship: A Cultural Account.* Chicago: University of Chicago Press.

Schneider, David M., and C. B. Cottrell. 1975. *The American Kin Universe: A Genealogical Study.* Chicago: University of Chicago Press.

Schooler, C. 1976. "Serfdom's Legacy: An Ethnic Continuum." *American Journal of Sociology* 81, no. 6 (May): 1265–86.

Schrag, Peter. 1971. *The Decline of the WASP.* New York: Simon & Schuster.

Schuman, H. 1982. "Artifacts Are in the Mind of the Beholder." *American Sociologist* 17, no. 1 (February): 21–28.

Shibutani, Tamotsu, and Kian M. Kwan. 1965. *Ethnic Stratification: A Comparative Approach.* New York: Macmillian Co.

Slater, Philip E. 1970. *The Pursuit of Loneliness: American Culture at the Breaking Point.* Boston: Beacon Press.

Smith, Robert, and Ellen Katzoff. 1986. *Content Reinterview Study: Accuracy of Data for Selected Population and Housing Characteristics as Measured by Reinterview.* PHC80-E2. Washington D.C.: Government Printing Office.

Smith, Tom W. 1980. "Ethnic Measurement and Identification." *Ethnicity* 7:78–95.

———. 1981. "The Subjectivity of Ethnicity." Mimeographed.

——. 1983. "Problems in Ethnic Measurement: Over, Under- and Misidentification." Paper prepared for the American Statistical Association, Toronto, August 1983.

Stein, Howard F., and Robert F. Hill. 1977. *The Ethnic Imperative: Examining the New White Ethnic Movement*. University Park: Pennsylvania State University Press.

Steinberg, Stephen. 1981. *The Ethnic Myth: Race, Ethnicity and Class in America*. Boston: Beacon Press.

Stevens, Gillian. 1985. "Nativity, Intermarriage and Mother Tongue Shift." *American Sociological Review* 50, no. 1 (February): 74–83.

Taeuber, Karl E., and Alma F. Taeuber. 1964. "The Negro as an Immigrant Group: Recent Trends in Racial and Ethnic Segregation in Chicago." *American Journal of Sociology* 69, no. 4 (January): 374–82.

Takaki, Ronald. 1987. *From Different Shores: Perspectives on Race and Ethnicity in America*. New York: Oxford University Press.

Tocqueville, Alexis de. 1835–39. *Democracy in America*. Translated by George Lawrence. Garden City, N. Y.: Doubleday, 1969.

U. S. Bureau of the Census. 1970. *Voting and Registration in the Election of November 1970*. Current Population Reports, Series P–20, No. 228.

——. 1979a. *Current Population Survey (November)*. Public use tape file. Washington, D. C.

——. 1979b. *Current Population Survey*. Interviewers Memorandum No. 79–18. November 1, 1979. Washington, D.C.

——. 1980a. *Census of Population and Housing, 1980: Ancestry of the Population by State*. Supplementary Report PC80-S1-10. Washington, D.C.

——. 1980b. *Census of Population and Housing, 1980*. Public use microdata sample C.

Van den Berghe, Pierre L. 1985. "Race and Ethnicity: A Sociobiological Perspective." In *Majority and Minority: The Dynamics of Race and Ethnicity in American Life*, ed. N. Yetman, 54–61. Newton, Mass.: Allyn & Bacon.

Van Esterick, Penny. 1982. "Celebrating Ethnicity: Ethnic Flavor in an Urban Festival." *Ethnic Groups* 4 (October): 207–28.

Weber, Max. 1921. *Economy and Society: An Outline of Interpretive Sociology*. Edited by Guenther Roth and Claus Wittich. Translated by Ephraim Fischoff. New York: Bedminster Press, 1968.

Weinfeld, Morton. 1981. "Myth and Reality in a Canadian Mosaic: Affective Ethnicity." *Canadian Ethnic Studies* 13, no. 3: 80–100.

Wilkinson, Rupert. 1988. *The Pursuit of American Character*. New York: Harper & Row.

Williamson, Judith. 1978. *Decoding Advertisements: Ideology and Meaning in Advertising*. London: Marian Boyais.

Winawer-Steiner, Hinda, and Norbert A. Wetzel. 1982. "German Families." In *Ethnicity and Family Therapy*, ed. Monica McGoldrick et al., 247–68. New York: Guilford Press.

Wirth, Louis. 1928. *The Ghetto*. Chicago: University of Chicago Press.

Yancey, William L. 1984. "The Structure of Pluralism: We're All Italian around Here Aren't We, Mrs. O'Brien?" Papers of the Albany Conference on Ethnicity and Race in the Last Quarter of the Twentieth Century. Albany, N.Y.: Center for Social and Demographic Analysis, State University of New York at Albany.

Yancey, William L., Eugene P. Ericksen, and Richard N. Juliani. 1976. "Emergent Ethnicity: A Review and Reformulation." *American Sociological Review* 41, no. 3 (June): 391–403.

Yankelovich, Daniel. 1981. *New Rules: Searching for Self-Fulfillment in a World Turned Upside Down*. New York: Random House.

Yetman, Norman R. 1985. *Majority and Minority: The Dynamics of Race and Ethnicity in American Life*. Newton, Mass.: Allyn & Bacon.

Yinger, Milton J. 1981. "Toward a Theory of Assimilation and Dissimilation." *Ethnic and Racial Studies* 4, no. 3 (July): 249–64.

Index

Compositor: Metro Typography & Design
      Text: 10/13 Sabon
   Display: Sabon
   Printer: Edwards Brothers, Inc.
    Binder: Edwards Brothers, Inc.